ELITE REAL ESTATE
PROFESSIONALS
TOP LEADERS IN THE INDUSTRY!

By

Elsa Palmer-Oden

Thomas Lalonde

Alina Chmielowski

Gerri Holgerson-Johnson

Krishna Mohan

Rick Premji

Dr. Klaus

Rick Donner

Moe Mathews

ELITE REAL ESTATE PROFESSIONALS

TOP LEADERS IN THE INDUSTRY!

Contents

CHAPTER 1
ELITE REAL ESTATE PROFESSIONAL ELSA PALMER-ODEN

The Virtual World for Investors

MY NAME IS Elsa Leigh Palmer-Oden. I am a wife, mother of two boys and an entrepreneur. I have had many different experiences in which I have learned many skill sets. My working career started at a young age working with my parents, building robots and filing paperwork. When I was in high school, I was in JROTC, which taught me leadership and self-discipline skills. I also started working at McDonald's. After high school, I moved on to being a convenience store clerk, which lead to store manager.

Over the years, I have also been a waitress, a service cashier at car dealerships, a clerk at auto part stores, a loan processor for auto and home loans, helped husband with remodeling jobs, and maintenance coordinator in aviation. All these experiences have given me a diverse range of experiences and skill sets.

In 2007 I learned of the term "virtual assistant", while looking for a legitimate work at home, or telecommute", a job for me to be able to be home with my boys after school. I finally found a legitimate virtual assistant staffing company to work with. Four years later, I quit working with the staffing company and started my own virtual assistant staffing company to assist real estate investors.

Throughout this process, I taught myself many ways to best keep my clients organized and the use of many systems to benefit our clients. Later in the year, I was introduced to a big name in real estate investing, and he introduced me as having "an army of virtual assistants" because I worked with several of his mentors and had trained a few people to help me. That is when my vision for helping people came to life! I now was able to train and contract many US virtual assistants, therefore getting to put people to work and help real estate investors grow their business in a cost-effective way. It has become a win-win for everyone.

Foreword:

Throughout this chapter you will learn the advantages, disadvantages, training, screening, and excuses of virtual assistants. I am writing this to open the eyes of real estate professionals, and other small businesses, to the advantages of having a great virtual assistant on your successful dream team! I hope you enjoy!

What Are Virtual Assistants?

Not that long ago, the term "Virtual assistant" was created by Thomas Leonard. He created this term in 1992 for his personal assistant that worked "virtually" for him. By 1998 virtual assistant training programs started to assist in the making of great virtual assistants. Even though virtual assistants have been around for over 20 years, the term "virtual assistants" is still a fairly new term to most people and businesses.

As technology keeps advancing, so do the skills and tasks a virtual assistant can do to assist an investor, or any small business, in their everyday needs. True virtual assistants are independent contractors, and entrepreneurs, who are given contracts with clients to provide professional administrative support. We used to refer to this type of "work at home job" as "telecommuting." Every year it becomes easier to work remotely due to the high advancements in technology. Virtual assistants work from home, with their own equipment and on their agreed upon schedule with the client.

These assistants do this type of work for various reasons. Some virtual assistants do this type of work because they are caregivers to sick or disabled family members, some have a disability themselves, while some homeschool their children or just want to have the freedom of working from home. A virtual assistant is also known as a "VA."

Virtual assistants come from many different backgrounds and, therefore, have many different skill sets in order to assist in many different ways. This diversity in backgrounds allows for small businesses to take advantage of the virtual assistant's skills to advance their own business. With the use of computers, internet, and online file and document sharing, there isn't much a virtual assistant can't do, other than what requires a physical presence. VAs charge by the minute worked or by specific projects. This saves real estate professionals, and other small businesses, quite a bit of money in office space, equipment, wasted time, insurance and taxes.

The Making of a Great Virtual Assistant and Types Of Virtual Assistants

The main difference in someone working remotely and still having to go to an office and a true virtual assistant that works 100% remotely, is the first is an employee and the other is an independent contractor. Some employees get the opportunity to work remotely, or telecommute, and are paid on a salary, therefore the hours actually worked aren't a concern to the company as long as the work is done.

A virtual assistant is an independent contractor who only gets paid for actual time worked, potentially saving the company a lot of money in wasted time, office equipment, office space, insurance and taxes.

You only want to contract a virtual assistant who can either be easily trained for your needs or one already trained for your business needs. This can sometimes be a difficult task. A virtual assistant needs to be very self-disciplined and able to multitask, in order to work from home efficiently.

Virtual assistants come from a large variety of backgrounds and cultures. You can find them all over the world, with all different skill sets and speaking all different languages.

Depending on the tasks you need help with, depends on the type and location of the virtual assistant you will want to contract. Any virtual assistant that you contract needs to be very self-disciplined from everyday distractions and be able to multitask efficiently.

These are not skills that everyone has! Many people are not able to keep from being distracted or are not able to multitask. They also need to have good computer skills as well as a good working computer and high-speed internet. Depending on the skills you need from your virtual assistant will depend on the other things to look for in your virtual assistant. Great virtual assistants usually have diverse backgrounds, but sometimes they are from one specific background that gave them the skills needed to assist others to grow their business.

Virtual assistants are independent contractors and therefore are their own boss. They have to have this mindset to be a great VA. The ones that have this mindset will be an asset to your team. The ones that look at this as just a "job" won't be as proactive and dedicated to assisting you, therefore they won't be as much an asset to your team. The assistants that have the right mindset are usually very proactive and need very little direction after the initial expectations have been set.

Communication is the key to success with any business and especially with virtual assistants. Without proper communication, it's hard to work virtually. You don't have someone down the hall to talk to and see things are getting done. In a virtual world, communication, trust and a system to keep everyone organized, is critically important for a successful relationship and for the most benefit of having a virtual assistant on your dynamic dream team.

You always want to make sure you have your systems in place when choosing a VA and choose a virtual assistant that fits your needs. There are many types of virtual assistants. Make sure to get the right type for your needs. Here is a list of some types and what to look for:

Phone VA : If you want your virtual assistant to make or receive phone calls, then they need to fluently speak the same language as the people they will be speaking with and they need to speak clearly. They will also need to have a good people person personality. It's always a good idea to use a virtual assistant from the same country where phone the calls are being made or answered. This avoids the cultural barriers between nations. For example, in the USA things are very different than they are in the Philippines. If a caller asks about a neighborhood or schools in the area, the foreign VA wouldn't know since everything is different there. Foreign vas can be used for phone work, but additional training and higher skill set would be needed for best success. These virtual assistants should also be doing texts too. Many people respond quicker with text than a phone call or voicemail message.

Technical VA: When you need a technically savvy assistant the location of the virtual assistant isn't as important as with a phone VA. With these types of virtual assistants, they just need to have the skills needed for the technical tasks you may need help with. This can be building databases or CRM systems, and many other backend technical things.

Basic Admin & Research VA: These virtual assistants can do any of your daily mundane tasks from data entry, scheduling appointments, proofreading, organizing emails and many other tasks including research. This type of virtual assistants doesn't need extensive training, only instruction as to the tasks you need. Basic vas are not necessarily specially trained in any one area and can be located anywhere.

Specialty VA: There are many types of specialty virtual assistants. These assistants don't need much training by you, only some direction and training of any special systems you may use. Some of the specialty virtual assistant fields are: legal assistant, scheduling assistant, real estate agent and/or investor assistant, personal assistant and event planning assistants.

Disadvantages of Having a Virtual Assistant –

Watch for the excuses!!

Whether working in a brick and mortar job or contract work, people are known to give excuses for not working or to cheat on time and work performance. In a virtual world, it seems the excuses can get even crazier than in the bricks and mortar world! I have managed bricks and mortar jobs and now the virtual community and have heard many crazy stories. I have laid out some of these excuses in this section, along with ways a virtual assistant can cheat you. This is for you to know what to pay attention to if contracting a virtual assistant that is not already being monitored. Very few companies like, Virtual Office VA Staffing, monitor and train the virtual assistants. Most virtual assistant companies don't do this and leave this on you, especially the foreign virtual assistant companies.

Some virtual assistants get too comfortable in their work, then, they get lazy and cheat on time and work performance. This is a big reason for the VA to always be watched and communicated with. Another great idea to control this is to have a system in place for them to use that timestamps their work. Google has docs, spreadsheets, forms, etc. that timestamp everything is done. If phone work is being done, use a system that logs all calls and duration of calls. If possible, also have calls recorded, at least periodically, so you can make sure they are doing everything right.

Virtual Office VA Staffing, LLC uses the Google document system and Vonage Business phone system to monitor all of this for you, but if you contract your own virtual assistant, you will want a system in place as well. Virtual Office VA Staffing also works with your CRM system (Dealflow, Podio, etc.) to keep it up to date. Other US-based virtual assistant companies make you use their system or they will only use certain systems.

Checklist of things to watch for with virtual assistant companies:

1. Prepayment for services - This can bring red flags. Are the prepayment hours really being used? Are you prepaying too much? Does unused (prepaid) time carry over to next month? What is covered in the prepayment?

2. Training - What is the skillset(s) that they specialize in? How much training have they received in what your needs are?

3. Monitoring - Is the virtual assistant's work monitored for accuracy with time and completeness of assignments?

When listening to recordings of phone work calls, you will want to listen for certain things in particularly:

- Do they sound pleasant on the call?
  - o Friendly, helpful, confident, etc.
- Did they ask ALL the questions you wanted or stick to your script?

- o Or did they skip through and "assume" some answers. I have seen this "assuming answers" numerous times.

- Are they hanging up after leaving a voicemail, or are they letting the clock run?

  - o This has happened. A virtual assistant left voice-mails then let the time on the call continue to run for a few minutes. This is considered "cheating time". Call duration times matched time being charged, but the voicemail calls were 4 minutes long, when the actual voicemail was less than 30 seconds! Hence, why Virtual Office VA Staffing monitors everything!

- Are they giving you accurate notes/information from the call?

  - o Make sure you have the virtual assistant supply as much accurate information notes as possible from any phone calls.

Now for the excuses. Time to have some fun! Just when you think you have heard it all, you will hear something else absurd. At Virtual Office VA Staffing, we handle these, so you don't have to listen to the excuses they give! I will list excuses here for you to know just how crazy these can get and for you to get a laugh. It's hard to always believe the reasons given because of how crazy the stories can get. Sometimes these are sad and true reasons not to work, but sadly those reasons are abused as well.

- "I can't work because I stuck my arm in a pot of boiling water."

- "I woke up in a field, not knowing who I was, where I was or how I got there."

*After being unresponsive for a few days.

- Another that was unresponsive for a few days, "I went to jail for the weekend, then released with an apology when the blood alcohol test proved I wasn't intoxicated." His VA Consultant happened to live in the same area and looked it up.

He wasn't in jail. Another VA knows his mother and found out he was just sick,

NOT in jail!

- " At the time I was supposed to work the accounts I was assigned to, I experienced a bit of a scare. My Facebook account had been hacked twice on two separate days, and the hacker was messaging a virus link to all of my close friends and family in an attempt to hack their accounts as well. One person took it upon themselves to report my page to Facebook customer service, and it was shut down as a suspected spam account, and I had to submit identification to recover my account." This took the virtual assistant 3 days to clear up and allow him to work again! His response about this being so important, "I know, I mean I know, it doesn't excuse anything but in my defense, doesn't having my Facebook account hacked constitute a feeling of panic? I mean I have a lot of friends".

- On first day to start making client calls, "My dog jumped out of 3rd story window and is on pain meds. I need to watch him and can't make calls."

Day 2: "My girlfriend had an asthma attack and I needed to be with her (no hospitalization was needed)."

Day 3: "My computer crashed and I need to get it fixed. It will be a few days." Three excuses in three days!

- " Omgoodness I've been having trouble with my internet all weekend... And to top it off I broke my cell phone. I dropped it into the tub on Friday."

- After a week of being unresponsive. "I am so sorry. I thought I had emailed you that I had the flu. I will be ready to start tomorrow, if that is okay. I promise to give 150%. I've been very sick. Crummy timing."

- This one may be real (not sure), but shows how everything can go wrong in your virtual assistant's life at once, even if you think you contracted the right person. " I did want to let you know that there was a death in my family, we have had to go to court on several occasions for my daughter as there has been very serious stalking threats not to mention we somehow ended up with a terrible pest control problem." "I can't work all the tasks this week because it's my birthday (or anniversary or child's birthday)."

- Reason for not working when agreed, "I set my shed on fire while boiling peanuts." This one was also a volunteer firefighter.

- After just 4 calls, " I can't do this job. I can't handle talking to any rude people."

- Legit excuses, but sometimes abused and lied about: "I'm sick.", "Family member is sick.", "Too many doctor appointments.", "I was in the hospital.", "Computer crashed.", "Internet has been out (multiple days).", "Lost power."

Do you have time to train, monitor and listen to excuses from virtual assistants? You don't have to deal with those headaches, because Virtual Office VA Staffing does it all for you! So, if you are looking to take your business to the next level, get a virtual assistant to alleviate the mundane tasks. This will allow you to focus on the more important things in your business and family life. I created Virtual Office VA Staffing to help you get real estate trained & monitored, US virtual assistants to assist you with growing your business. The programs include local to your phone numbers and a customized system designed around your needs, at cost-effective pricing.

Virtual Office VA Staffing thrives at taking investors to the next level in their business. Whether new to the industry or a seasoned investor, virtual assistants can always make your life easier.

For a great US virtual assistant - Call 855-2-GET-A-VA or visit our website: www.REIAssistant.com .

ELSA PALMER-ODEN BIO:

MY NAME is Elsa Leigh Palmer-Oden. I am a wife, mother of two boys and an entrepreneur. I have had many different experiences in which I have learned many skill sets. My working career started at a young age working with my parents, building robots and filing paperwork. When I was in high school, I was in JROTC, which taught me leadership and self-discipline skills. I also started working at McDonald's.

After high school, I moved on to being a convenience store clerk, which lead to store manager.

Over the years, I have also been a waitress, a service cashier at car dealerships, clerk at auto part stores, a loan processor for auto and home loans, helped husband with remodel jobs, and maintenance coordinator in aviation. All these experiences have given me a diverse range of experiences and skill sets. In 2007 I learned of the term "virtual assistant," while looking for a legitimate work at home, or "telecommute", job for me to be able to be home with my boys after school. I finally found a legitimate virtual assistant staffing company to work with.

Four years later, I quit working with the staffing company and started my own virtual assistant staffing company to assist real estate investors. Throughout this process, I taught myself many ways to best keep my clients organized and the use of many systems to benefit our clients.

Later in the year, I was introduced to a big name in real estate investing, and he introduced me as having "an army of virtual assistants" because I worked with several of his mentors and had trained a few people to help me. That is when my vision for helping people came to life! I now was able to train and contract many US virtual assistants, therefore getting to put people to work and help real estate investors grow their business in a cost-effective way. It has become a win-win for everyone.

CHAPTER 2

INTERVIEW WITH ELITE REAL ESTATE PROFESSIONAL
THOMAS LALONDE

P*LEASE INTRODUCE YOURSELF* **and a brief thumbnail of your background.**

My name is Thomas Allan LaLonde, Jr., but my friends call me Tommy. I am a husband, father, entrepreneur, professional engineer, self-proclaimed dreamer, and a bit of a nerd. Above all, I am a Christian. I am married to my high school sweetheart, Tammy. Together we have two kids, Brooke and Blake.

I was born in Lorain, Ohio as the middle of three siblings. I moved to Texas in 1975, and have lived here ever since. Growing up, I took every opportunity that I could to learn "hands-on" about topics that interested me. I was the kind of kid you'd find swinging a hammer, cutting wood, taking apart the family lawn mower and hustling to cut the neighbors' yards to earn a quick dollar. When something peaked my inquisitive nature, I literally could not sleep until I understood how it worked. I guess some things never change.

I am a graduate of Texas A&M University, Class of '94. I own multiple small businesses in North Texas, including a structural engineering and home inspection company, a soil remediation company and one of the oldest drainage and irrigation companies in Dallas Fort Worth. I applied my experience in soils, structural performance, and problem-solving to create the business model for my latest endeavors, Happy Buy Homes, LLC and Lease to Buy, LLC – real estate investment companies.

Describe what drives you and your passion to do what you do and help the people you help.

I am driven by an internal force that compels me to be in constant pursuit of knowledge, and to use that knowledge to help others solve a problem in a unique way.

My passion for learning and creative problem solving first led me to be an engineer. For at least a decade, I worked directly with property owners helping them identify and mitigate foundation problems. After several years specializing in soil mechanics and structural performance, I decided to leverage the bright minds in my organization along with my understanding of structural design and construction to find houses with "good bones" in need of cosmetic repairs – so we started a real estate investing company and construction company. While flipping houses in my "spare time," I witnessed a huge problem that demands a creative solution. Sometimes, when it comes to real estate, people get stuck. I use my creative problem-solving skills to find wiggle room so we can get them into a new home, or help them out of a home that is causing an emotional or financial strain.

Can you share a lesson you learned early on, that still impacts how you do business today?

As children, we are taught many lessons. Don't run with scissors or you will poke an eye out. Don't play with fire or you will burn the house down. Don't spend too much time daydreaming, because it's not practical. Don't say what is on our mind, because it may not be socially acceptable. Well, I have always marched to the beat of my own drummer and I've never fit into any mold. People often tell me that I can't do things, or I can't do things the way I want to do them. If there is one thing that I have learned, it's that there is more than one way to skin a cat. For every problem there is a solution. I always ask myself, "Is this the best way to accomplish my goal, or am I choosing the path of least resistance?" Asking that question every day helps me break out of complacency and challenge the boundaries that restrict people from the dream of homeownership.

Please tell me about any recent business accomplishments that you are most proud of and why?

In addition to owning Thomas Engineering Consultants, in 2001 I acquired Lee Engineering Company, one of the oldest irrigation and drainage companies in Dallas Fort Worth. This acquisition provided my team the opportunity to utilize one of the most respected irrigation and drainage companies in North Texas as a platform for better education to property owners on the importance of proper irrigation and drainage as it pertains to one of their most important investments – their real estate property. With the destructive nature of our highly expansive soils in North Texas, homeowners find themselves spending over a billion dollars a year in foundation repairs. Through the education efforts of both Thomas Engineering and Lee Engineering, I became the pioneering engineer in North Texas to design and implement the use of dedicated foundation watering systems to reduce the seasonal movement of our structures which is saving property owners millions of dollars per year in unnecessary structural repair and water costs. Today the team at Lee Engineering is recognized as the leading authority in foundation preservation utilizing custom foundation watering systems as well as water conservation technologies and Thomas Engineering continues to exemplify the standards that are expected from a professional engineer. We hold paramount the safety, health and welfare of the public. We strive to comply with the principles of sustainable development in the performance of our professional duties, and we speak out against contractor abuses towards property owners.

With our teams in place on the engineering side, most of my time is now spent with my real estate team at Happy Buy Homes. Together we help homeowners from every background, and all walks of life, manage their personal battles and freedoms with homeownership. Everybody deals with joy, pain, illness, sadness, financial stress and many other emotionally straining situations at some point in their life. Our goal at Happy Buy Homes is to understand all of the variables impacting the lives of our client and to develop the greatest emotional and monetary solution possible for our client.

As a real estate investor, it used to seem that helping solve one person's problem in real estate was only a small win for that one family. But when I began to consider the chain effect of everybody who benefits from solving that one family's problem, then that one win becomes more significant. I recognize that the accumulative wins become a monumental accomplishment. When I think of the people I serve and help on a daily basis, I am overcome with joy and satisfaction knowing that I am able to touch somebody's life in a way I never before imagined possible.

What Leadership qualities in Leaders do you most admire and why?

Every great leader should be willing to learn and rebound from their mistakes. He/she should be committed to improvement, while remaining humble during times of triumph. I admire leaders that think outside of the box. I believe that most situations are resolved by using critical thinking and creative problem-solving. The best leaders find answers by reading in between the lines and pulling out solutions.

My leadership style is transformational. I seek to inspire my employees by creating a warm, yet stimulating work environment to promote effective communication and intellectual stimulation. I'm all about investing in my employees, and I'm not afraid to commit company time and resources to advance their training and education. The way that a CEO interacts with his employees is a direct reflection of the stability of a company.

What has been a key element of your success?

Each of my companies are backed by hard-working individuals, who are like family to me. Every CEO says their employees are like family, but I take it to heart. These are the people that I surround myself with every single day. We raise our families with one another. We laugh together. We've cried together. When one of us struggles, we all struggle. When we succeed, we celebrate our triumphs together. I am so very blessed to surround myself with such a talented, flexible, genuine group of people. I owe much of my success to those who have stood by me each time I get a wild hair and decide to open a new business. I could not do what I do, if not for their willingness to keep learning! In the same regard, I am blessed to have my tirelessly supportive wife, Tammy, and my children to keep me grounded. They remind me why I work so hard. Coming home to them at the end of each day is the highlight of my life.

That is what it all comes down to though, isn't it? Surround yourself with good people, hold true to your values, and NEVER lose your childlike sense of wonder and enthusiasm for learning. I want to be a part of something great, and I want to share that with my family and my team.

What inspired you to become a Real Estate Investor?

I wanted to help people achieve homeownership on their own terms. One major element that fueled my passion for real estate occurred during my pursuit of off-market listings. I frequently met homeowners in terrible situations. Many were drowning in debt and overwhelmed by their circumstances.

Often, they felt like there was no way out. I will never forget one family in particular. The conditions that they were living in were unimaginable. Sewage lines around their home had malfunctioned for years, causing leakage within the crawlspace of the pier and beam foundation. Over time, the excess moisture wreaked havoc on the structure, causing the foundation to shift and the subfloor to crumble from constant duress. The soil beneath the flooring, drenched with overflow from leaking sewage pipes, was visible through gaping holes. The odor coming from beneath the home was an assault to my senses. Stepping through the narrow hallway to the bedrooms, I felt a sickness in my stomach and wondered, how did they survive in these conditions? How long had it been like this? The rotted subfloors were littered with rodent droppings. My heart sank when I thought about the children living in the home. The homeowners had fallen into a state of depression, knowing they could never afford the repairs it would take to get the house in livable condition. The stress of their situation had taken a toll on their lives. They were in over their heads and thought they'd never find a way out. The homeowners were expecting me to walk out, having seen the condition of their home. Anyone in their right mind probably would have hit the pavement running. Luckily for them, I don't think like everyone else. I didn't run away like every other investor had done for the previous 6 months. Instead, I made an offer for their house in as-is condition. We closed the deal a few weeks later. I'm happy to say that they took the cash and were able to purchase another house in much better condition. I didn't give this family any charity, and they didn't do me any favors either. We were able to work out a deal that worked for both of us, and that is what I do. I help homeowners get out from under unwanted real estate so they can move on with their lives.

What area of real estate investing do you do?

I work with motivated sellers, non-motivated sellers, and even renters who need creative assistance to realize their dream of homeownership. I also work with everyday people to provide solid returns on retirement money secured by real estate.

Motivated sellers are usually facing divorce, foreclosure, have liens against their home, or numerous other circumstances that require them to sell their home quickly. My team is trained to react in lightning speed to these types of sellers, because they are generally working within time constraints.

On the other hand, a non-motivated seller may be someone who has inherited an unwanted property, has a lot of equity in their home and are considering selling, looking to downsize, or maybe they are tired of being a landlord. When a homeowner wants top dollar for their property and doesn't need to sell it in a hurry, we consider them to be a non-motivated seller. A lot of investors won't work with these types of sellers, but we have flexibility and can often times make an offer that is full asking price, or very close to it.

We also work with people who want to own a home but may have some credit or job-related issues holding them back. They may have been turned down for a mortgage loan and think their only option is to rent. We help people just like this get into a house they can afford, in their desired location, and on their way to becoming a homeowner.

Finally, we work with all levels of people who are tired of see-ing hard-earned money sitting in a bank account making very little interest. I see so many families burdened by the realiza-tion that their retirement savings aren't sufficient. It is a terrible thing to watch the money in your elderly parent's bank account erode and you wish you could have done something about it. I recently met with a man who put this reality in perspective for me. He has a lot of money in the bank, but he was deeply concerned that if he has any health issues that require tapping into his savings, then his money could be gone in a few years. He was tired of seeing his bank account generate less than 1/4% interest, and traditional investing was too much of a roller coaster to risk his money. He was genuinely at a loss. He reminded me of why I have a passion for helping others. So, part of what I do is work with people in all stages of their life who want to see their hard-earned money grow at a better than average rate of return through good quality investments secured by real estate.

Describe at least one big problem you specialize in solving.

It is very common for people to be stuck between a rock and a hard place when it comes to real estate. Whether they want to sell, need to sell, or just need help qualifying for financing, I use creative solutions to problem solve on their behalf.

Alright, this is going to get deep for a second, but bear with me. There is a theory on human motivation called Maslow's Hierarchy of Needs. I think about this theory all the time because for me to help people, I must be able to understand their needs and empathize with how they are feeling.

This theory states that a person's physiological needs must be met before they will be able to pursue happiness or fulfillment at a deeper level. Physiological needs include the unchanging demands that are required to survive, such as food, water, and shelter. How does this apply to what I do?

PROBLEM: A family lacks adequate shelter because they don't have a home, or maybe their home is falling apart and they can't afford repairs. They must obtain this basic necessity before they can direct attention to other needs such as belongingness, esteem, family, and even their own health.

SOLUTION: I have systems in place that allow me to make a cash offer on the property and close in a very short period of time. They won't have to make any repairs, pay any fees, or spend months hoping and praying that their home will sell.

The second level of Maslow's Hierarchy is the need for safety. Once a person's physiological needs have been met, they can begin to focus on their health, well-being, financial security, and personal security.

PROBLEM: Your real estate seems like an endless money pit. The stress is so overwhelming that it is affecting your health and relationships.

SOLUTION: Get a fair price for your real estate, close the deal quickly, and move on with your life! It is easier than it sounds, I promise.

I am passionate about helping homeowners secure these basic needs; the physiological need for adequate shelter, safety needs for health, well-being, physical and financial security. I have witnessed men, women, and children living in a house that is crumbling around them because they can't see a way out financially. The moment I rid them of the burdensome property, it is like a tremendous weight is lifted off their shoulders. No longer overwhelmed by their circumstances, they can move forward with their lives and advance to the next levels of the hierarchy. They have more energy to devote to social belonging needs such as friendship, intimacy, and family. They are free from the emotional baggage that was attached to the property and can begin rebuilding their sense of confidence, esteem, and self-respect. Witnessing the transformation of families as they go through this process is the most rewarding aspect of my business.

How are you different than your competitors?

I think that real estate investors get a bad reputation for having a lack of compassion. While there are certainly plenty of investors that are just looking to make a buck, I always ask myself,

"Is this what is best for the client?" and "Does this deal align with my values and business goals?" If the answer is yes to both questions, then the deal takes place. If not, then I politely move on.

When I first got into the industry, I received a voicemail from a woman in tears. In her message, she stated that her house was in foreclosure and going up for auction the following Monday. She heard that I might be able to stop the foreclosure and decided to give me a call. It was already Thursday evening. I stopped everything that I was doing to try to make it work. Unfortunately, I didn't have the staff in place to work within that tight of a timeline. After that night, I worked diligently to put the processes in place so I could help the next person who left a message like that on my answering machine. Sometimes, it can be hard to know when to throw in the towel. As time passes, it becomes clear that circumstances have changed and things aren't going as planned. People reach out to me when real estate costs them too much financially or emotionally. I will crunch numbers, and find every resource available to come up with a solution.

Describe the outcome that can be achieved by working
with you?

I will keep working to come up with a solution that works for all involved parties. I want everyone to leave the transaction satisfied that they were treated fairly and happy that I could help them.

Not everyone is trying to unload their real estate. I get a lot of calls from homeowners who have taken great care of their house and want top dollar for it. Often, they are surprised at what we can offer them. On the other hand, there is a long list of reasons why people may suddenly need to sell their real estate. Some of which include homeowners facing divorce, foreclosure, property liens, illness, death, unwanted inherited properties, etc.

Then there are the massive numbers of families that are unable to obtain a traditional mortgage to own a home. These types of buyers are tired of throwing money away renting, but need a little help getting approved. I put pen to paper to find a way to get them into a house and working towards the American dream of owning a home.

What are some of the business projects that you are currently working on that you are excited about and why?

I am honored to be in a position to reflect on the journey of the past 25 years of my adult life. Authoring my first book has been a sobering reminder that God gives each of us the opportunity to experience life on earth only once. Life is not intended to be a solo experience. Every decision we make and every action we take molds who we are as a person and the impact we have on those around us. The bonds that connect each of us are often thought to be bigger than life itself. I am so very thankful for the opportunities God has given me to connect with new people every single day. Whether it be through Thomas Engineering Consultants, Lee Engineering Company, Happy Buy Homes, or Texas Lease to Buy, every day is just one more day that I have the opportunity to make a difference.

How can folks get in touch with you?

You can reach me by shooting an email to office@happybuy-homes.com or office@leasetobuytx.com. If you'd like to talk to one of our property specialists, call 817-345-6444. You can also visit our websites at www.HappyBuyHomes.com and www.LeaseToBuyTX.com.

THOMAS LALONDE BIO:

Thomas Allan LaLonde, Jr., P.E. is a husband, father, entrepreneur, professional engineer, self-proclaimed dreamer, and
a bit of a nerd. Above all, he is a Christian. He is married to his
high school sweetheart, Tammy. Together they have two kids,
Brooke and Blake.

Tommy was born in Lorain, Ohio as the middle of three siblings. He moved to Texas in 1975, and has lived here ever
since. Growing up, he took every opportunity that he could to
learn "hands-on" about topics that interested him. He was the
kind of kid you'd find swinging a hammer, cutting wood, taking
apart the family lawn mower and hustling to cut the neighbors' yards to earn a quick dollar. When something peaked his
inquisitive nature, he literally could not sleep until he understood how it worked - some things never change.

A graduate of Texas A&M University, Class of '94, Tommy owns multiple small businesses in North Texas, including a structural engineering and home inspection company, a soil remediation company and one of the oldest drainage and irrigation companies in Dallas Fort Worth. He has applied his experience in soils, structural performance, and problem-solving to create the business model for his latest endeavors, Happy Buy Homes, LLC and Lease to Buy, LLC – real estate investment companies.

CHAPTER 3

INTERVIEW WITH ELITE REAL ESTATE PROFESSIONAL
ALINA CHMIELOWSKI

Please introduce yourself and give a brief thumbnail of your background.

Sure, TC. My name is "Alina" Chmielowski, and I was born and raised in the Philadelphia area. I'm married to my high school sweetheart, and we have four children.

After graduating with honors from Drexel University with a degree in Chemical Engineering (the top woman in my class), I went on to work for a major corporation. Within a couple years, I made my way to the think tank of the company to evaluate new technologies. Although I absolutely loved my high-paying engineering career, I felt like the Lord was calling me to home-school, so I left all that behind to focus on our growing family until they were older.

What a blessing that sunny Florida has been our home for the past 10 years. During that time I have been able to pursue my interest in the martial arts, earning three black belts in karate and one in Kobudo (weapons).

Prior to dealing in real estate, I used my skills to tutor in mathematics, chemistry, and physics. One of my students was able to significantly improve his SAT math score which earned him a full scholarship to the college of his choice. Helping my students achieve their goals is very satisfying. *Amazing results are the bottom line.*

Wow, four black belts! Tell me more about that.

Practicing the art of karate requires many hours of training, a great deal of discipline, and awesome teachers like Sensei José Arias. Over two years ago, Shihan Lynn Kureth of Minami Dojo in Naples named me a sensei (teacher) which is an honorary title bestowed on only a few select black belts and carries with it great responsibility. It's kind of funny because all the other senseis are males in their 20's who have been studying since they were children. I'm incredibly honored to be a fellow sensei with those talented young men. Following the earning of my first black belt in Kobudo, I was allowed to study multiple Okinawan weapons. My favorite is the katana, a Japanese sword.

So what made you switch from engineering to real estate?

While the two career paths may seem to have nothing in common at first glance, there's actually a skill set overlap. Obviously, engineering requires an analytical mind, but so do many aspects of real estate. Also, it's enjoyable for me to help others by finding solutions to their difficult problems, whether it's evaluating the feasibility of a new technology or finding the right buyer for a homeowner. Real estate also gives one the opportunity to eventually earn a passive income, a subject which interests many people.

Describe what drives you and your passion to do what you do and help the people you help.

Striving for excellence is just part of who I am. No matter what I do, I always do my best because I do it for the Lord. He has blessed me with certain gifts and talents which are supposed to be used in service of others, whether it's in engineering, private tutoring, or real estate.

Can you share a lesson you learned early on, that still impacts how you do business today?

The focus of any business, whether it provides a product or service, should be understanding the needs of its customers and then meeting or exceeding those requirements. Making the customer happy is what truly matters.

Please tell me about any recent business accomplishments that you are most proud of and why?

Being invited to write a chapter in this exclusive book has been a tremendous honor. I appreciate the opportunity to share my story with others so they would know the person with whom they'd be working. The decision to move can be one of the biggest and sometimes scariest decisions in life. It's nice to know that someone has your back when you need to sell your home.

What leadership qualities in leaders do you most admire and why?

Leading by example, leading by challenging one to do better, leading with humility... these are some of the characteristics I most admire. Another key quality I admire in a leader is being solution-oriented. When one is in a crisis, worrying about the problem doesn't help. Finding a realistic solution does. *Again, it all boils down to getting results - amazing results!*

What has been a key element of your success?

Not only meeting, but exceeding, the expectations of my clients is the key to success. I always strive for excellence in all that I do. *The motto regarding my customers is: "You deserve amazing results!"* Hence the name of my company, Sugoi Enterprises LLC. Sugoi is the Japanese word for amazing.

What inspired you to become a Real Estate Investor?

Although many avenues exist for supplementing one's income, real estate offers the highest rate of return if executed properly. It's also a lot of fun!

What area of real estate investing do you do?

Right now, I'm focused mainly on wholesaling because it allows one to enter the real estate world with little to no money. It's a practical way to get one's foot in the door. Pun intended! ☒

Describe at least one big problem you specialize in solving.

My specialty is helping homeowners who need to sell find cash buyers so they can close quickly with peace of mind.

How are you different than your competitors?

To be sure, many other men and women are very good at their jobs. However, my ability to network and make the appropriate connections benefits my clients directly. I'm here to help in all aspects of the transaction and won't disappear after closing.

Describe the outcome that can be achieved by working with you?

By working with me, sellers can feel confident that their cash closing will happen quickly and smoothly. Investors can be assured that I will find them the best off-market deals possible. Together, it's a win-win situation for both sellers and buyers.

What are some of the business projects that you are currently working on that you are excited about and why?

Aside from this incredible book, I'm also working with a builder to help him market custom homes in southwest Florida. As more snowbirds are coming to the area, it's a fabulous way of fulfilling a need for second homes. They're also great for first time home buyers, as well as those who can't find their ideal home.

How can folks get in touch with you?

Name: Alina Chmielowski
Company: Sugoi Enterprises LLC
Phone: 941-500-2954 (call or text)
Email: alina.chmielowski@gmail.com
Website: homedealsinswfl.com

ALINA CHMIELOWSKI BIO:

BORN AND raised in the Philadelphia area, I graduated with honors from Drexel University with a B.S. in Chemical Engineering. This 5-year program involved three 6-month co-op assignments interspersed throughout the years of study. I was fortunate enough to work for such chemical industry giants as Rohm and Haas and E.I. du Pont de Nemours and Company (now DowDupont Inc.), as well as a local refinery. Following graduation, I was hired at Air Products & Chemicals, Inc. and earned my way to a position in the think tank of the company where my responsibilities included, among many other cool duties, evaluating the technical feasibility of various new technologies. For one of the projects, I was recognized for my contribution in saving the company over $9 million. Amazing results are the bottom line.

While I absolutely loved my high-paying job for which I had worked so hard to obtain, I felt the Lord calling me to homeschool. So that's exactly what I did! I left my career behind to focus on our growing family and actively volunteer in our church. Ten years ago, my husband and I moved our four children from the woods of Pennsylvania to the palm trees of Florida and began a new adventure. At that point, with the children now in private school, I re-invented myself again, this time as a private tutor specializing in mathematics, chemistry, physics, and SAT prep. Because I was able to help one student dramatically improve his math SAT score, he was awarded a full scholarship to the college of his choice. Amazing results are the bottom line.

Always learning and growing, I was finally able to pursue my longtime interest in the martial arts, earning a total of four black belts in both karate and Kobudo (weapons). One day, I plan to travel to Japan to train as well as experience their beautiful culture. To that end, I'm currently studying the Japanese language, including its four different writing systems. In 2015, I was given the honorary title of sensei (teacher) which is reserved for only the most dedicated and talented black belts. Again, amazing results are the bottom line.

Recently re-inventing myself once more, I'm now delving into the intriguing realm of buying, selling, and flipping homes in the SWFL area. My appreciation for the Japanese language inspired the name of my real estate investing company, Sugoi Enterprises LLC. "Sugoi" is Japanese for "amazing", and I believe all my clients deserve amazing results.

CHAPTER 4

ELITE REAL ESTATE PROFESSIONAL GERRI HOLGERSON-JOHNSON

HELLO, MY NAME is Gerri Holgerson-Johnson. I was born and raised in Massachusetts. And in 1990, my husband decided to change jobs, he made a business investment that required not only a large amount of acreage, it required a farm-sized acreage. So, we packed it up and headed west, or rather, northwest to South Dakota with one son and one very fickle grouchy cat. We lived there for 6 years before an epiphany struck us that there was no real reason to live where more months of the year were cold and frozen than not! We sold the business and land, packed up again and moved to sunny

Southwest Florida in 1996 with two more sons, two dogs, three cats and a hamster named Mutt. Since then I've been a full-time resident. Prior to that, since the late 70's, we vacationed on Marco Island long before Marco Island was a well-known vacation destination. Boy do I wish I had understood real estate investing at that time!

I am currently an active licensed Florida real estate agent and budding real estate investor. My interest in real estate started over 30 years ago when my husband taught me how to evaluate property for our eventual home. At the time I had no idea that real estate would become a passion of mine. But that's the second part of the story ....

My dad spent most of his life in either construction, roofing or remodeling homes in Massachusetts and around the country.

However, he wasn't the one who influenced me the most – it was my Mom.

She planted the basic seeds of renovation and design when I was a child. When I was 7 we moved into a two-bedroom, one bath apartment in a 12-unit tenement building built in 1905. Back then the bathrooms consisted of a tub and a toilet. I think the space wasn't more than 4 feet by 5 feet. The only luxury feature about that bathroom, other than it was at least indoor plumbing, consisted of a now much sought-after cast-iron ball and claw tub! There was a small walk-in closet sized un-insulated cold storage room at the end of the kitchen which left barely any room for the kitchen table.

The first lesson that I remember about creating better living spaces came from that apartment. My mom had the vision. She saw a dining space in that cold storage room and a three-piece bathroom by replacing the tub with a shower and adding a small sink. Hooray! No more brushing teeth in the kitchen sink! She brought her idea to the landlord who loved it and he agreed. The rent went up of course....

And my introduction to remodeling and renovations had begun the memories of which I had tucked away until sitting and thinking about writing this chapter. Along the way she also taught me how to paint and wallpaper. She had grit, willpower, vision and style and I feel that I carry that with me now.

My years of experience through hands-on learning has led me to design, create and manage anything from basic updates to full home remodels on property over one-million dollars. Through the years I have studied home staging with a prominent NY designer whose method is incorporating the client's own furniture, as well as, the basics of Feng Shui and energy house clearings. My life in "real estate" has led me down many paths of knowledge and growth and I feel that I bring these abilities and qualities forward in all my endeavors.

What drives me now and that I am passionate about is helping a client looking for a new house and finding them a HOME! When clients have a clear and distinct vision of what they want, without any extraneous financial or credit concerns and very few possible roadblocks, the home search and buying adventure is pretty easy and flows smoothly from start to finish. However, that is not generally the situation. Challenging situations of all sorts appear that you would not anticipate, at least I didn't. I had one transaction for an elderly woman who only spoke Spanish, is bed-ridden, had no internet and therefore no computer and lived across the state. The situation came with additional obstacles like a purchase price well under $100,000.00, which in many areas of the country may not be a tremendous issue, however that is not the case in southwest Florida. She also has two dogs that are on the

"dangerous" list, so that meant no gated communities or communities with rules excluding them. The woman's relatives who live on the west coast of Florida found me at an open house one afternoon just as I was finishing for the day. They are relatives of the elderly woman and were in charge of finding the new home. They were frustrated, stressed and tired. In addition, they had been stood up by the agent that they thought was working with them. Due to the rules and law of ethics, if they had signed a Brokerage Relationship Contract with the other agent, I would not have been legally or ethically able to work with them. They assured me that they hadn't. They told me their situation and I told them very honestly that between the issues with the dogs and price point considerations, while maybe not impossible, they were at the very least challenging. The only thing I promised was to do some research and let them know what I found. Frankly, I was not optimistic about finding anything in their price range that wouldn't need at least that amount again to make it livable. However, their story touched me, because it was apparent that their love and passion to find a better, safer home for their elderly relative was of utmost importance and needed so they could easily care for her. I called Jon to ask if he knew of any property in their price range that would work with creative financing, unfortunately nothing was available at the time. I bugged all my friends and contacts that sometimes have investment properties hoping for anything that would work. I then consulted other agents, in case they knew of anything coming on the market but not yet listed on MLS. When asked the price point, I was told I was crazy, that my effort would not be worth it, to drop it and just move on. How I could I do that? When I got my license to sell real estate it was because I believed in one thing, helping people who want and need our help. My instructor always said, if you do your part right, the money will follow. But I digress ...

I scoured our MLS and Craigslist and Facebook Marketplace and anyplace I could think of and the pickings were very slim. When I found a few properties that were the best I could find and truthfully, slightly above what they had to spend, I called and told them what I found, and we made appointments for showings. It was then that they finally understood that the price point was going to be a major issue and finding a suitable safe home that didn't need tens of thousands to repair was going to be next to impossible. They consulted with their relative and a decision was made to double the price point!

Well, as the story progresses, the house that was chosen was new construction and the only way to create a sales contract was online! No exceptions! Believe me, I begged and pleaded with the sales office to let me print it and mail it to my client! Ultimately, since there was no internet at this woman's home, I did the only thing left to do that would get the contract put together; I had to drive across the state. I got lost due to construction and hung up in rush hour traffic and finally met with the client's daughter who interpreted the sales contract and we got it done! The listing agent was shocked that I went to such lengths, especially considering the sales price! Everyone in their sales office said, "Honey, you've earned this commission"! LOL...

I could have quit or referred them to another agent, however I was nervous that another agent would turn them away as well. I'm glad I didn't quit. The transaction continued to be fraught with credit issues, timing issues and almost anything that could go wrong, did. The sale finally closed, with credit to a mortgage broker who I called to explain the exact circumstances they were up against. She later told me that my personal contact to her caused her to go above and beyond to assist. I am very grateful to her. I feel a great sense of accomplishment and reward knowing I didn't quit and that this wonderful woman has her family close by to care for her and a safe and lovely place to call home.

The lessons I learned early in life about doing my best, treating people with respect, doing the right thing even when it's hard or inconvenient or challenging beyond limits, have a good work ethic, be an ethical person, pay attention to detail, all comes from my Mother and I owe her the greatest debt of gratitude. She was always the best at whatever she put her mind to accomplish and went above and beyond to treat people well. Her legacy to me wasn't through the riches of money, but through the riches of character and those are the attributes and qualities that I feel govern how I do business now.

Long before being licensed a real estate agent, I've had an interest in personal growth, which lead me to an interest in coaching and leadership. Through that I have learned how I best learn for retention and use of what is learned. As an adult with ADD, it takes a lot of repetition for me to really get a concept down pat. As a result, the main qualities that I look for in a leader, trainer or coach are those who understand that everyone does not fit into any one specific method of learning. I've learned to align myself with those that have these qualities because I know that I will get the kind of attention and training that I need to learn, the way I learn and retain information. Since meeting Jon, Stephanie and

Lisa, I know that they understand that too. They teach by example, work with a person individually or in a group and help them develop the tools for success. AND they make it fun! Because of my experience with prior coaches and trainers I've learned that being told that I MUST adhere to a strict method of doing things and that it is the only way to be successful, doesn't work for ME! Anytime I hear that, I know I am in the wrong place.

My inspiration and desire to become a real estate investor, as I've mentioned earlier started over thirty years ago, long before the internet was what it is now, and my research was provided by scouring real estate sections in newspapers and the real estate magazines found in kiosks on street corners. I would imagine the interiors or visit open houses, daydreaming about what I would do to improve them.

I was very busy raising my family back then and had to put this idea on the backburner. It wasn't until the advent of HGTV and all home renovation shows plus the plethora of extremely expensive investor training workshops and seminars that caused me to think about it again since my family is now grown and I now have the considerable time it takes to start and finish a project. I have a new opportunity to follow the road back and start again. Currently I own one rental property with plans to own more within the next few years. I'd say I am definitely in the rookie season of my real estate investment career. The area of investing that interests me most is multi-units or larger homes with multiple bedrooms for college rentals. My second and more important goal concerning real estate investment is to teach my sons the value of real estate investment for themselves. And how to use that to create great financial freedom for themselves and their families.

If I could share a few suggestions with new investors who enjoy "flipping", as that is my passion too, remember to not over improve or under improve a property. Don't take on the most expensive house in a neighborhood or improve one to the point of creating the most expensive house in a neighbor-hood either. Carefully evaluate where to spend the big renova-tion dollars and how to use creative choices to extend the bud-get. If the choice is between all new kitchen and bath cabinets with granite countertops but the flooring will be mismatched room to room due to budget constraints, consider refacing the cabinets instead and use another countertop surface. There are many ways to find used cabinets from

The Home Store or Craigslist to save money. When I go into or find recently "freshened" or renovated houses online and see new tile in some areas that doesn't match the rest of the house, I know the investor has wasted his/her money. Pay attention to trends but don't necessarily live by them. But stick to some of the basic, classic design details. Nothing will date a house faster than cramming in as many current trendy ideas as possible. KISS is a very accurate way to approach any redesign or renovation. Be aware of the current paint color trends, but again, keep it simple. If a designer white is more budget friendly you can add that trendy pop of color using accessories, even if it's only the color of a plant in a pot or tow-els in the bathrooms, do that if you are not going to have the property staged for sale. Also, if you are not sure about your decisions, get some advice. Preferably from someone like me. I'm pretty good at this.

What I'd like to share with new real estate agents, research who you want as your broker. We all know how saturated the market is with agents so ask around. Make sure to choose someone who is passionate about their business, loves to see people succeed and wants to and will provide extensive train-ing. Choosing a non-competing broker is best. Always pay for professional photos for your listings.

Photos of knick-knacks on shelves or toilet seats left up instead of a great photo of the entire living room or excellent shot of the bathroom, aren't the pictures that sell a property. Look online, you know what

I'm talking about. If you are taking a listing for a client and it's a mess, take the time to explain to them that, more often than not, buyers cannot see beyond clutter or dirt. Help them pack it away if necessary. You want them to achieve the best and fastest results, don't you? Please, use spell check to create the best professional image for yourself. By law, you must be affiliated through a brokerage, however this is Your personal business, a vocation you have chosen for yourself, take the time to proof read your material to present yourself in the best most professional way for success. I personally pass over listings that contain several spelling errors. If that agent isn't concerned enough to care about spelling, what else do they not care enough to do properly? Learn everything you can about accurate pricing because the homeowner's ego is in charge when you go for a listing appointment and you can miss the opportunity for a quick sale and closing if the home is overpriced. Trust me on this, I had to learn the hard way! It is to your ultimate benefit as a professional to guide and educate. And keep learning. Clearly this is a vast subject and I've been allotted only a finite number of words for my chapter in this book, but the last piece is of prime importance, be safe. When you are showing property or hosting an Open House, always let another person know where you are and what time you expect to be there or be done and make plans to contact them within a specified time or have them contact you.

Take whatever precautions you can think of. While this advice is generally focused toward female agents, I feel this is just a good business and security practice all around. Stay safe my friends!

It wouldn't be right to leave out the subject of problem-solving which is a major component to a successful transaction whether you are a realtor or investor or just among the living. Now, I cannot claim that I necessarily excel or specialize in problem-solving. However, I am particularly clever AND extremely good at reaching out to those who know more or have been doing it longer, better and more than I have. Problem-solving many times requires thinking outside of the box or going above and beyond to make the transaction happen. I've been greatly blessed with great friends like Cat Oswalt and

Kathy Holbrook who are also real estate professionals that I admire and trust, and mentors like Jon and

Stephanie Iannotti and Lisa Donner that are truly delighted to help another person succeed. If problem

-solving is not a strong trait of yours, find the people in your circle who are and cherish them!

Clients ask from time to time how I'm different than my competitors. How am I better than the others, how do I set myself apart? Because of our current technology and access to hundreds if not thousands of ways to showcase a listing for sale or find a desired property, the competitive playing field as I see it, is pretty level for the most part. Even though all my clients have been word of mouth referrals, every client comes with expectations that I try to meet or exceed, in some cases anticipate and be ready with an answer or solution. I have learned that staying in contact with a client, keeping them apprised of market conditions and counseling/coaching them through the inevitable stressful parts, anticipated or otherwise, has been my most advantageous strategy. A few additional skill sets that I have up my sleeve are using the fundamentals of Feng Shui to make suggestions to clients in ways that are easily implemented without being overwhelming. I am also able to do energy clearings for homes, property and businesses. It is always beneficial to do a clearing of a home before, during and after the sale, after renovations or prior to moving into a new home. Home staging is also one of the ways clients benefit from working with me. What I like about the home staging training that I received is that is does not require getting rid of the items you already own and love but uses them to create a new more enjoyable living space without a lot of expense. I will also consult with clients who are looking to redesign their space, whether it is choosing new tile or wall color, appliances or any components that go into a remodel or renovation.

I find that communication is a major factor in creating a strong bond between myself and my clients.

They benefit from working with me because I help them define what they want. Sometimes they know exactly what they want other times it takes talking it out, defining the details to get on the same page. I help guide and educate them if they have concerns or issues that need clearing up before we begin their home search and offer them contacts and possible professionals to choose from to achieve their main goal of home ownership or investment.

While I do not consider myself a Super Star real estate agent, investor or business person Yet, I feel that I am finally in the right place at the right time and aligned and associated with the right trainers and professionals to create the success that I want at the level of success that I dream of. The thrill and anxiety of being asked to participate in this book of real estate professionals that have already created levels of success that I dream about, when I am just at my beginning stage, is to me, a major boost to my confidence and a complete thrill. I am forever grateful for the faith, trust and confidence Lisa, Stephanie and Jon have placed on me in their invitation to participate.

I thank you for taking the time to read my chapter.

God Bless.

If you would like additional information regarding any areas discussed in my chapter, I can be contacted through Bronze Flamingo Investment Group, LLC., at: bfig.info@gmail.com

GERRI HOLGERSON-JOHNSON BIO

I'M ORIGINALLY from Massachusetts and raised in Lowell. I now live in Bonita Springs Florida with my husband and two Shui tzus. Throughout high school, I never had a clear thought or direction to what I would do with my life. After high school I attended two semesters of college before realizing that I had too many areas of interest and I struggled to settle down into just one. I had worked summers and part-time since I was 14 years old, so I chose to continue working until I could decide on a course of action.

I then took a job as a bank teller, advanced to the position of branch manager and assistant treasurer where I wrote the first set of teller and customer service representatives training manuals that were implemented company-wide. I continued my banking career for 10 years before starting a family.

I was extremely fortunate to be a stay at home mom for my three sons. We moved a couple of times from Massachusetts to South Dakota and finally settled full time in Florida.

Along the way I had the opportunity to successfully renovate and sell several homes before considering real estate as my next career. While I am an active, licensed Realtor, I've existed more under the cover of Secret Agent rather than as a Super Star Agent, which then led to my interest in investment real estate and becoming involved with the Florida Gulf Coast Real Estate Investment group.

I am currently finishing a whole house remodel with my husband Randall and see myself moving toward simplifying many of my other interests, so I can focus on building a strong investment portfolio.

CHAPTER 5

ELITE REAL ESTATE PROFESSIONAL KRISHNA MOHAN

MY NAME IS Krishna Mohan.
I currently own and operate three businesses in Retail, Real Estate and Business Consulting. At the same time I am also working on acquiring businesses as a part of our growth strategy. I have many years of experience as a successful Senior Business Leader and my background is in, among many other things, Business Development, Sales Team Training and Management, Key Account Relationship Management and International Business. My in-depth understanding about business comes from extensive experience in working in Manufacturing, Consumer Durables, Telecom, Information Technology, Energy and Data Center industries.

My Education background is in Business. I have Master's Degree in Marketing Management MMM, MBA-International Business (USA) & MS-Finance (USA)

In the 20-years I've worked with 3 Fortune 500 companies and several start-up organizations in Sales, Business Development and Finance. I have achieved definitive and long-lasting outcomes in Team Leadership, Information Technology, Data Center Consulting, Client Relations, Strategic Planning, Product Marketing, Managing Key Account Relationships and have generated millions of dollars in annual profits. I have exceeded organizational goals while driving company growth, developing new business and delivering sustainable financial results.

Others have characterized my professional management style as decisive and motivational where success comes from a focused commitment to developing new business, cultivating relationships, training salespeople and creating growth strategies. I also have extensive involvement with start-up operations, RFPs and C-level negotiations.

I am very passionate about my work and I am keenly interested in the three main elements that companies need in order to succeed: Business Development, Finance and Sales. Of course, I believe that sales are the driving force of truly successful businesses and without a substantial amount of them the company will undoubtedly fail. Companies must be fully aware of the importance of the other two also. Without Business Development a company will not grow and understanding how Finance impacts costs, taxes, depreciation, etc. will only help it to move forward in a consciously controlled manner.

Psychologically

Since the most valuable tool a company has to increase its Revenue is Sales, it is imperative that clearly defined Sales procedures are set in place and that they can be easily duplicated. Each step of the Sales process must be documented for future salespeople in the company.

If it works – don't fix it – document it.

Sales is interesting to me on a number of different levels. They can be looked at from a psychological point of view in the sense that the salesperson must know who he or she is dealing with. You must discover the customer's profile, define the ideal persona of the prospect and use it as a map that will ultimately help you close the sale.

Is this person my prospect?

Qualifying the prospect is very crucial to avoid wasting time and expediting the closing process. You must ask yourself, "Is this person my prospect?" Well, if you are selling expensive cars or yachts and the person makes only $7 per hour then most likely you will be safe in taking him off your potential prospect list or taking him out of your 'funnel.' On the other hand, you should know upfront that if you have 100 prospects in your funnel that probably 70% of them are never going to buy from you even though their profiles fit the bill.

In direct sales when you suspect that someone might be your customer you can tell a great deal about the person by just watching for a brief period of time. What does his face tell you? Where did he buy his clothes? Does he spend a lot of money at happy hour? Of course, the only way to find out where he goes for happy hour is to actually talk to him at some point without trying to sell him anything.

Sales Cycle

High-end product sales, many times, take a long time. Once you know that then you prepare yourself for the long game. Some Sales Cycles take well over a year, while others may only take a day or a week or a month. Having an understanding of this approach will save you lot of frustration and will prevent a lot of good salespeople from quitting. Many business owners become disappointed because sales are lagging. In reality, however, they are actually disappointed because they don't know the Sales Cycle of that product or customer. If you know the Sales Cycle and you know the customer's profile – then you can't fail. You must also know the customer's need.

What Does The Customer Need?

How does one find out a customer's need, you might ask? Since we're still in the psychological area of actively exploring who this prospect really is, we can step it up and move the whole investigation into the 'detective' stage, which is certainly related. That's what a friend called it, anyway, and it makes sense. We mentioned finding out where he goes to happy hour but what about the rest of his life, where else does he spend time? During that initial conversation with the prospect, you may have found out where his happy hour is, if he's married and has kids and if he belongs to a club. These things are not national secrets and if approached in an unthreatening way, most people will tell you almost everything you want to know. They do that because they are human and they are thrilled that you, who are not selling anything to them, have taken a genuine interest in them. It's human nature and you are just having an innocent conversation with someone. You are also having a conversation with someone who may only be paying partial attention to you. He may be texting someone or scrolling down his messages on his smartphone or he may be watching the big screen TV on the wall behind the bar. He has to have a reason to pay full attention to you. An important point to remember is that if you are the only one talking the prospect may in all likelihood lose interest and want to leave. He may have decided that he simply didn't like you because you talk too much.

You must let the prospect talk about himself and you should practice being a good listener. Let him ask you some questions so he can research you instead of just vice-versa. Once that happens, trust begins to build on the part of the prospect and he will probably approach you the next time he sees you. There is no hurry at this point because you already know that it's the long game, so there's no need to be desperate. Best case scenario you made a friend and closed a sale. Worst case you did not close business but you made a friend. He can in turn refer you to his friends. Just get to know a new friend and enjoy yourself wherever you are. Closing the sale will come later.

So, if they go to a certain club, you may want to join that club too. That way, you can talk to your prospect more often. Remember, this is the long game we're talking about, the kind that has a long Sales Cycle. If it was a short Sales Cycle, like a day or a week or even a month, there might be less expensive ways to 'bump' into your prospect than joining a club.

Super Sleuth

You know that the prospect belongs to the club, but who else is a member? Are there other salespeople who go there on a regular basis? You should explore the club and go for a few visits if possible, to see for yourself if your competition has beat you to the punch. This type of selling can be a lot of fun. You'll find that once you assume the attitude of a salesperson who is also a super sleuth it puts you into a whole other category than the average salesman who is simply looking for a quick sale. You will find that you are more aware of your surroundings and that you do things in a more conscious way. You will also find that besides being more cognizant of yourself and your environment that you are also developing a more empathetic nature, just by being aware of the things you used to take for granted.

The ideal for any sales person and especially for the people in high-end sales is to be the only salesperson in a room that is full of prospects. Seasoned salespeople know exactly what I'm talking about here: Opportunity! However, manifesting that ideal is like getting everything you ever wanted as gifts on your birthday. It's a nice thought but it only rarely happens. Not to discourage anyone because I said rarely – not never. It could happen to you. Check out your prospect's club and if there are other salespeople who go there too, that just means that you have to work harder to get the sale. Getting a prospect in your funnel is an opportunity that shouldn't be wasted.

Funnel

We've talked about going after one prospect but we don't want to give the impression that a sales professional should drop everything and focus only on one specific prospect. Your funnel should be full before you start working on any prospect. That is part of the process: prospecting. Ideally, you should have a hundred potential prospects on your list (funnel). Once you do that then you can go out fully confident in the knowledge that many of the potential prospects will not turn into prospects or sales but there is enough in your funnel that can carry you to success without having to go back to cold calling or hunting down potentials in any other way.

Your funnel is your ammunition and it should be able to last through many sales pitches and closings. The funnel, filled with prospects Information and statistics is the tool that can move you forward in the world of sales. If you only have one or two potential prospects in your funnel you don't want to run off and start selling. You'll be out of people to call or visit in about ten minutes if you even last that long. Preparation is the key to sales and preparing your funnel with the best prospects you can find is what true professionals do – then they begin their sales campaign. There is an old story of two men who were given axes and hired to cut down two very thick trees – one tree each. One man immediately went over to his tree and started swinging his very dull axe at the trunk. The other man looked closely at his chopper and calmly walked over to the blade sharpener and began to hone his axe. He took twenty minutes to put an edge on it and when he was done he looked over at the other man who was sitting in the dirt breathing heavily and totally exhausted. His tree had barely been dented by his edgeless axe and he wore himself out with nothing to show for it. The man with the sharpened tool cut his tree down in record time and wasn't even sweating when it fell over. Thorough and solid preparation can make all the difference in the world when it comes to sales or cutting down trees. Never take your funnel for granted.

You can always refresh your funnel when it starts getting low but you'll be surprised at how well a fully stocked funnel serves you and your approach to sales. Each prospect in the funnel is a treasured asset – until it is not treasured any longer. That, of course, is when you KNOW that a sale is not going to be made to a specific person.

Credibility and Trust

Who are the best salespeople in history? That's right, the ones who have credibility and are trustworthy. Credibility and trust are the two traits that bring in more sales than anything else. Who sells the most cars on the lot? The guy who is believable and who people trust. Credibility and trust. Who sells the most yachts? The salesperson who found the customer's need and is believable and trustworthy. Credibility and trust. We could go on and on but you get the point.

Credibility and trust work in every part of your life. The reason there are so many negative jokes about used car salespeople is because somewhere, sometime in the last one hundred years there was a pattern of bad behavior that permeated many used car dealerships across the country. Obviously, not all used car salesmen are untrustworthy but once the rumors started spreading they never stopped and we have all those bad jokes about them today.

If you have credibility and trust, you are halfway to closing the sale. You should also position yourself for success in life. That is, even if you lose the sale you will gain something valuable. You will learn something that you may not have ever learned if you got that sale. You need to gain something even if you fail. That is winning also. If you make the sale – you win. If you lose the sale you must gain something, therefore you also win. It may be that by losing the sale you have gained a friend in that former potential prospect and who knows what could happen with that? One of his friends may become your prospect and you win again. That kind of thinking or positioning keeps you emotionally and mentally healthy and it makes you more aware of what you are doing and how to do it even better the next time.

Do and Learn

Most people just do and they don't learn. That is, I am constantly learning when I am not doing. I do, but I also learn. The man with the dull axe was a doer and not a learner. The other, more successful tree cutter was obviously a doer and a learner. The simple point behind this observation is if you only do – and aren't constantly learning, then you will be left in the dust of those much more enterprising people who want to constantly up their game and become the best salespeople in the history of the universe. It's that simple. They do, no doubt, but they also learn. They learn by watching successful salespeople in action to see what they are doing that makes them better than everyone else. They learn by reading – about everything so that they converse with any prospect on any topic and not come up short or appear to be unread. Do and Learn.

The Mind

Everything happens in the mind and then it happens in reality. What does that mean? It means that our CPU (Central Processing Unit) our mind is really running things. It is running our lives, it's keeping us in the cycle of debt that many of us can't seem to escape and it's running our careers – our sales life. The mind is also pushing us (perhaps unconsciously) toward failure because we don't believe in ourselves and it is also driving us toward success because for some reason, we know we were cut out for the big money and we know we can make that and any other sale. "I knew he meant Yes, when he said No." Some people might think that is overconfidence and even a huge over-grown ego, but it actually works for a number of people who are willing to play the long game in sales. One sales professional met with a buyer for a chain of department stores. The buyer turned him down at the first meeting and he came out very confident knowing that the buyer would eventually say "Yes.' Six months later, after stopping at the store once a week to say "Hi" to the buyer he got all of his products accepted into the chain. Of course, he had profiled the buyer and got to know him and found his need (the store's need). He also learned about the chain and he was extremely credible and trustworthy. He also knew that the buyer was his prospect and that he was only one of a hundred prospects in his funnel and that he might lose the sale at some point. He recognized that the Sales Cycle was a long one and that time was on his side and that he was also willing to lose the sale in order to get the sale. He also was well aware that his product added value to the store and its customers, which brought him even more credibility and trust in the eyes of the buyer.

There is No Competition

There is no competition. There is abundance in everything! There are so many people who are looking for exactly what you have to offer, but you just don't know who they are yet. Walk the path that no one else walks. Life has a purpose. These are some of the things I believe in when it comes to sales and when it comes to life itself. Life does have a purpose – and it's up to us to find that purpose in our own individual lives. If we look around we might be able to recognize that many people have different purposes in life, that is, each one has something that drives them that is different from other people around them.

And that is fine, at least they are lucky enough to have found real purpose in their lives, which is something a lot of people can not say. I believe that each one of us has a purpose and that eventually we will find out what that is. I also believe that we are surrounded by abundance and that we need to each learn how to enjoy it. There is no competition. Yes, that is true. It goes back to the workings of the mind. With this mindset we need to design the product, solution and be a trusted consultant to the prospect. We need to focus all our energies in helping the client and not worry about competition. What is your mind telling you at any given moment? Is it telling you to be fearful or whispering in your inner ear that competition surrounds you and is going to eat you up? What if your mind, rather, what if you let your mind tell you the truth: that there is really no competition and that those kinds of negative thoughts are only an illusion? Wouldn't that be something? There is no competition because you are the person in front of your prospect and what he sees is credibility and trust and nothing else. The implication here is that in reality we control our minds and what it tells us at any given moment and I choose to give my mind permission to tell me that there is no competition.

Winning

I believe anything we want to accomplish happens twice. Once in the mind and then in reality. We need to use the subconscious mind and start practicing winning in the mind. Having a firm belief in the outcome combined with action will lead to victory. I believe failure is an option and winning is a Choice.

KRISHNA MOHAN BIO:

KRISHNA MOHAN has a deep grasp on the understanding of business through his extensive experience working in Manufacturing, Consumer Durables, Telecom, Information Technology, Energy and Data Center Industries. He is a highly successful Senior Business Leader who also has a background in, among many other things, Business Development, Sales Team Training and Management, Key Account Relationship Management and International Business.

Over the last 20 years he has worked with 3 Fortune 500 companies and several start-up organizations focusing on Sales, Business Development and Finance. He has achieved definitive and long-term outcomes in Team Leadership, Information Technology, Data Center Consulting, Client Relations, Strategic Planning, Product Marketing, and Managing Key Account Relationships and has generated millions of dollars in annual profits.

His management style has been described as decisive and motivational where success comes from a focused commitment to developing new business, cultivating relationships, training salespeople and creating growth strategies. He also has comprehensive involvement with start-up operations, RFPs and C-level negotiations.

Krishna holds a MMM-Master's Degree in Marketing Management, an MBA-International Business and an MS in Finance. He currently owns and operates three businesses in Real Estate, Business Consulting and Retail.

CAPITAL STREET INVESTMENTS LLP is global investment Management Company whose team of experts is committed to real estate investment that is research driven. Capital Street's intrinsic values and long-term prospects enable the company to acquire real estate properties and commercial buildings that bring substantial value to its clients and investors. www. capitalstreetinvestmentsllp.com

GENIUS VISIONARY INC a Global Business Consulting firm started off with a vision to create a productive business environment that helps entrepreneurs to reach their goals. From business coaching to Acquisition advisory we cover everything in between.

www.geniusvisionaryinc.com

GIFTING BOUTIQUE LLC offers a unique shopping experience for those special customers who are in need of personalized gifts to suit individual taste. In addition Gifting Boutique specializes in designer women Fashion Accessories and Clothing. Gifting Boutique is known for designing most unique styles and products in the fashion industry.

www.giftingboutique.com

CHAPTER 6

INTERVIEW WITH ELITE REAL ESTATE PROFESSIONAL RICK PREMJI

Q: Please introduce yourself and a brief thumbnail of your background.

M Y NAME IS Rick Premji, I am married and have 3 wonderful children ages 9, 7 and 5. I have a bachelors degree in Commerce. I've been in the retail business since 1997. I had a successful convenience store /gas station in Tennessee. I had several jewelry stores in Tennessee and Maryland area. I've been a financial advisor since 2014 and have been in Real Estate since 2012. One of my biggest achievements is being invited to participate in this book.

Q: Tell us about your Real Estate Properties and how you are helping your Clients.

The properties that we are interested in is single family minimum 3 bed 2 bath medium price range plus or minus 50% in any city in America. Traditionally, this is what the average American is looking for in a home.

How we are helping our clients is that we are a service company that helps sellers sell their house in only a few days by buying it. We network with different companies in the area and when their Executives or Employees move in town we put them into our houses.

We offer alternative ways for sellers who don't want to sell their house Traditionally and don't want to go through the hassle of fixing the property, listing it and then showing the house to a bunch of strangers.

Q: Describe at least one big problem you specialize in solving?

We help people resolve their situation by working with them to come up with a win-win solution.

I will say we help people to help themselves, solve their problems. Everyone has a different situation, so we try to provide solutions for their individual needs. There is no one solution to every situation, and we provide a custom-tailored solution according to their need - whatever it may be. Sometimes people think it's the money but it's not true it could be something else. Sometimes they think it's their ugly house or they have to move because of a new job, it could be family issues or health problems, we help people to find out the reason why are they selling it and try to solve it in the best way possible for them.

Q: Describe the outcome that can be achieved by working with you?

The outcome that can be achieved by working with us would be that they will have a SOLD House. The seller can move on with their life. Sometimes real estate is a big issue that rips families apart, they cannot live with their family because the house is not sold or they have find their dream job but they can't move because of an unsold house. There could be several different situations that they are stuck in, we help them to achieve their goals, so they can move on with their life. We show them how they can benefit when they sell it to us and help them go towards their destination.

An example is one of our sellers, Myrna was in a situation that she couldn't wait 6 months to sell her house she called us and was very happy with the outcome this is what she said.

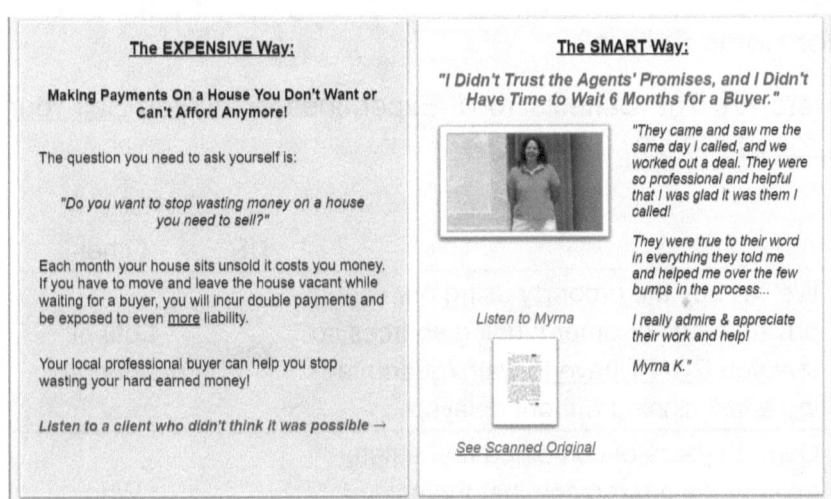

Describe the difference in achieving this outcome can make in their life?

Everyone has a different outcome depending on what their situation is. Here is an example of the Clark family. They were skeptical in the beginning and thought it too good to be true but now they are happy that they called and we were able to solve their issue. This is what they had to say

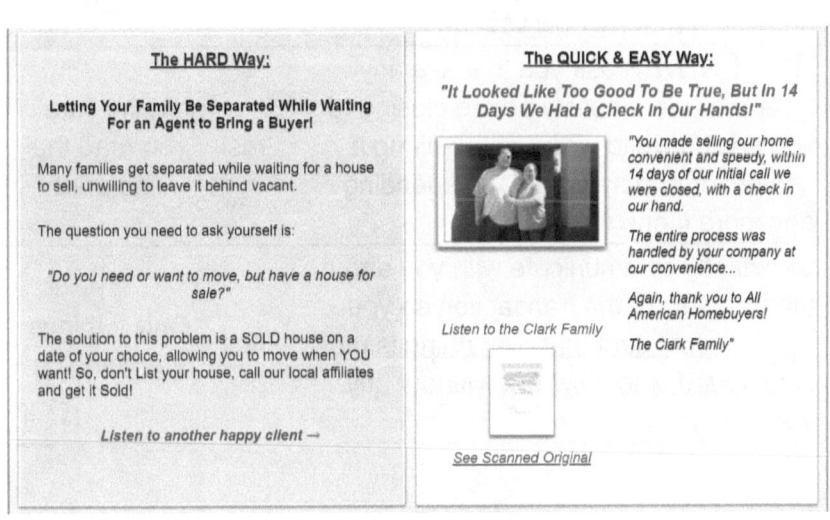

Q: What are the advantages of selling their home quickly for Home Sellers?

Here Are The Benefits You'll Experience When You <u>Sell Your Property To Us</u>

	US	Other
We will buy the property using our cash, private funds or other funding sources so that <u>you DON'T have to wait.</u> (guaranteeing a fast closing without delays)	Yes!	Lots of contingencies
Over 20 years of combined real estate experience guarantees that the sale of your property goes as smoothly as possible	Yes!	Who Knows?!?
Team of the best title agents, attorneys, and professionals all working to get your home (you'll <u>feel confident</u> everything is done 100% correctly)	Yes!	Most of the time a "one man" show
We will buy your property WITHOUT having to move the tenants out of the property (and risk the closing not taking place and your property now vacant)	Yes!	Will want the property vacant
We will NEVER ask you to make any repairs to the property before closing (so you don't have to worry about hiring a contractor or handyman and spending any more money)	Yes!	Make sure you read the fine print
Constantly communicate with you about the progress of the transaction so you can <u>feel confident that everything is</u> <u>moving forward smoothly</u> (and without any surprises)	Yes!	Only if things are going ok

We will have the transaction handled by a licensed and insured title agent so that you can rest assured that everything is being done above board.	Yes!	Be careful
We will ensure that you have the proceeds from the sale of your property the day of closing (so <u>you can get the cash for your property immediately</u>)	Yes!	Read the fine print
You will NEVER have to pay any real estate commissions or hidden fees (so you'll know exactly what you'll get once the sale is done)	Yes!	Read the fine print
Move on the day you want (you decide when you want to move out)	Yes	Move when they want

Q: What do you feel are the biggest myths out there when it comes to homeowners to sell their home quickly?

There are several myths that I feel are out there when it comes to homeowners to sell their home quickly.

Myth #1 – How much is the house worth?

Something we hear all the time is that the seller says "I know how much is the value of my house". Sure, the home seller will be the one making the final decision as to what price the house will sell for! However, contrary to the home selling myth, the actual selling price will be subject to market conditions, the property's location, and its size! Many home sellers might be of the impression that they're sitting on a gold mine, because their family and friends have said that. Whereas they all have the best interest at heart for the home seller, with all due respect, they won't be the ones buying it, but they all become a real estate pricing experts. The home seller probably is the least of all suitable for pricing his own property, as he's too emotionally involved and will obviously hope to get more money out of it than what it's worth! This may sound a bit harsh, but unfortunately, these are the facts.

Myth #2 – A quick offer means the property's priced too low

When they get a fast offer, they think they have priced the property too low! They think they're giving their home away. There could be other good reasons as to why offers came in that quickly!

Myth #3 – You can completely depend on online valuations

Does Zestimates ring a bell? Some property portals believe that their algorithms can outsmart the traditional valuations. The reality is that they have yet to do that. Depending on the geographical area, Zillow's Zestimates prices can be off by 20% to 30% and this is a big concern about correct home prices. Because of this, the home sellers has a false expectations regarding the valuation of their home. There are just too many variables which can affect the valuation.

Q: What are some common misconceptions about the Real Estate Industry?

The common misconceptions about the real estate industry are people think that everyone in the real estate industry is a used car salesman. The investor only wants to rip me off, or they only want to pay 50 cents on the dollar or they want to steal my property - but it's not true. We like to create a win-win situations and try to give them a fair market price. We do buy some properties at a discount when it needs repairs, but we also pay full market price or sometimes more depending on what the sellers needs are. Sometimes the seller wants fast cash and sometimes they can wait and agree on terms.

Q: What are some of the most common fears about selling their home?

Actually, some common fears about selling their home are that they don't understand the process of selling the house, what it takes to sell the house. They need to learn and understand the process. Sometimes they think that it's beyond their ability to sell it by themselves or they are scared -what if it doesn't sell. When they call us we explain the process, try to find what they want and if we are a good fit for each other and the property fits our criteria we buy the property, if not at least we will educate them in the process.

Q: How can they get past these fears?

You past your fears by facing it. Because when you face your fears you'll see there was nothing out there. It is something that you believe in your head so once you do face it you realize they weren't there.

Q: What other perceived obstacles do you see that might be preventing home sellers from seeking the help of a Real Estate Investor?

The Obstacles that I see that might be preventing home Sellers from seeking the help of a real estate real estate service company like ours is that they think we will give them a lowball offer, that we will take their property for pennies on the dollar. What I think is the seller should be realistic, for example if they have a $5 bill and they want $6 dollars, why is somebody going to give them six or seven dollars for the $5-dollar bill? What if it's a $5 bill and they want to sell it for $5, why would someone be interested in a $5 bill for $5? Somebody would be interested if they sell the $5 bill for $4.50 or maybe they will become the bank and give that person time to pay back the $6.

Q: What are some of the little-known pitfalls or common mistakes you see Home Sellers make on the road to sell their home quickly?

Mistake No.1: Getting Emotionally Involved

Once you decide to sell your home, it can be helpful to start thinking of yourself as a businessperson and a home seller, rather than as the homeowner. By looking at the transaction from a purely financial perspective, you'll distance yourself from the emotional aspects of selling the property that you've created many memories in.

Mistake No.2: Expecting To Get Asking Price

Any smart buyer will negotiate, and if you want to complete the sale, you'll have to play the game. People should list their homes at a price that will attract buyers while still leaving some breathing room for negotiations. This will allow the buyer to feel like he or she is getting a good value and allow you to get the amount of money you need from the sale. Of course, whether you end up with more or less than your asking price will likely depend on how much they like your house and how well you have staged your home.

Mistake No.3: Trying to Hide Significant Problems

Any problem with the property will be uncovered during the buyer's inspection, so there's no use hiding it. Either fix the problem ahead of time, price the property below market value to account for the problem or list the property at a normal price but offer the buyer a credit to fix the problem. Realize that if you don't fix the problem in advance, you may turn away a fair number of buyers who want a turnkey home. Having your home inspected before listing it is a good idea if you want to avoid costly surprises once the home is under contract.

Q: What inspired you to become a Real Estate Investor?
Q: Can you share a lesson you learned early on, that still impacts how you do business today?

I will be honest, financial independence was the first inspiration for me to come in real estate because I have seen more financial independent people in real estate than in any other industry and second that I can help people. I see that people have situations and I can solve their problems for them and it make satisfying for all involved. I try to create a win-win situation, because they will sell if it makes sense for them and vice versa we will buy if it makes sense for us, so it has to be a win-win for everyone. The number 1 lesson I learned early on was to be honest and try to give them the best advice for their situation and sometimes that could be that we are not a good fit for each other. People will know that you are trying to help them and not take advantage of them.

Q: What's the most important question home sellers should ask themselves as they consider selling their home?

- They should ask themselves who is my competition?

- They have to see other homes for sale in the area and ask themselves these questions.

- What is the price they are selling for?

- Why are they selling for that price?

- What do they have to offer that I don't?

- How can I show the buyer benefits of my house?

Q: What's the most important thing home sellers should consider when evaluating a Real Estate Investor?

I think when you meet with them you should ask yourself is he trying to help you solve your issues and concerns? Is he trying to solve your problems? Is he honest with what he has to offer, and is it a win-win for everyone? If the answer is yes, he is someone you want to work with!

Q: How can someone find out more about Rick Premji and All American Home Buyers and how you can help?

To find out more about us, see if we are a good fit for each other and we can create a win-win offer for your house, or if you want to learn more about real estate passive income you can contact us:

All American Home Buyers
Rick Premji
(423)999-5000
website: Rickbuyhouses.com

When you call us and mention this book I will send you a free report that reveals

"What you must know if you want to sell your house quickly and avoid costly mistakes!"

RICK PREMJI BIO:

My NAME is Rick Premji. I came to the USA in 1996 and I have been married to my beautiful wife since 2006. We have 3 wonderful children ages 9, 7 and 5.

I have a bachelors degree in Commerce. I've been in the retail business since 1997, owning multiple jewelry stores in TN and MD. I had a successful convenience store /gas station in Tennessee and liquor store in AL. I've been a financial advisor since 2014 and have been in Real Estate since 2012. I got into real estate in order to help others and have financial independence for my family.

CHAPTER 7

ELITE REAL ESTATE PROFESSIONAL DR. KLAUS

The alchemy in Real Estate

The inside road to transferring DIRT to GOLD

"All that we are is the result of what we have thought. The mind is everything. What we think we become."

— Gautama Buddha

IN THE BEGINNING there is always a thought to start a career in Real Estate. It starts for most when a seed is planted inside you by watching an add on TV or reading the newspaper, on social media, by "finding" a book in the library or bookstore. Sometimes by attending a meeting of local Real Estate Investors.

These "gurus" of Real Estate always offer introduction workshops for a quick and easy way to wealth, in the past I saw these classes offered by Ron LeGrand, Russ Whitney, Robert Allen, Lou Brown, Kris Krissner, Kathy Kennebrock, Ray Higdon and others.

These Gurus have done Real Estate Investing and now they are teaching the method they have been successful with and are offering their method.

During the workshop there is always a sale pitch for tools, upscale classes, coaching, virtual assistant, DVD's or books to make the path easy and without any roadblock to become a Real Estate Millionaire by harvesting the low hanging fruits. These done-for-you-systems can cost up to $120,000.00 today.

In the beginning of my investing career I attended the classes of Ron LeGrand after I bought his "How to be a Quick Turn Real Estate Millionaire" and became one of the first Masters of the Financial Freedom Academy. Back then it was very affordable.

Another Guru spoke at a meeting of Ray Higdon's Real Estate Investing Group, Lou Brown. He offered a different approach to Real Estate Investing and Asset Protection, which I found very interesting and added his system, special Land trusts, to my toolbox.

All these systems are a big toolbox for me and I pick a tool I want to use and think about how I can tweak it workable for my idea. As I consider myself as an outside of the box thinker, for example I still use very successful a handwritten postcard instead of the famous "yellow letter". Using this method I was able to find, hold and flip a lot of Dirt and created a big basket of Gold Nuggets.

During the financial crisis my gold mine dried out as the prices dropped steady as Seller still wanted Top Dollar because of their mortgage. Because these mortgages the houses were underwater, the market value was less the mortgage, the new solution appeared to be a Short Sale, unfortunately the Bank's and or the Mortgage Servicer stalled the process, either by stating they are unable to do something until the Homeowner is as a minimum 90 days late on payments or when a short sale package was faxed to the servicer, it was never received.

One time I faxed the package 18-times and finally I was told there is foreclosure lawsuit filled and file moved to the Foreclosure Department.

Frustrated I looked into my big Toolbox and as a result I developed the Quiet Title Workshop in connection with lawyers because of all the issues from Mortgage Electronic Registration System to fabricating documents by third parties and the unwillingness of the Servicer to name the owner / investor of the note.

For several reasons I found it necessary to transfer the deed to a Land trust and therefore I invited Lou Brown to speak at my first three workshops about the advantage of a Land trust, as he is a recognized expert of using trusts for Real Estate Investments.

One way to realize the quality of the Quiet Title Workshop Curriculum is that State BAR's in several States approved the workshop for Continuing Education Credits.

One of my niches today is research for the Chain of Title and to analyze recorded documents. I am able now to explain to a lawyer with knowledge why I want to do a Quiet Title in a different way as he would normally do for an investor with an Tax Deed Certificate. The Gold Nugget is passive income from Rental Properties.

Before the Financial Crisis started with the bankruptcy of "Lemon" Brothers and in a domino effect banks were closed by the FDIC, at any given event hundreds of people showed up to become a Real Estate Investor. Astonishing for me attendees bought all these home study courses and workshops in a heartbeat. It sounded so easy, money was available even for a "German Sheppard" to buy a spec home, credit card limits were raised by just asking, even home equity lines were applied for over the phone with no appraisal necessary. It seemed like Real Estate is a Gold Mine without doing any digging, you bought a house with no money down and 100% financing, the appraisal came in higher than contract price, next month you flipped it and received a nice check at the closing table. Sometimes no financing was necessary, in a simulate closing you closed the house with the money from the resale.

To fill seats most presenters offered a money back guarantee up to the end of the second day or full return of the tuition was offered when a deal was finalized in the first 6 months after the event.

It appears I was one of few whoever requested a refund at a event. I did that at the Real Estate Marketing Workshop with Richard Roop & Dan Doran. The handling of my refund was not as promised " no question asked", instead I was forced to wait for Dan Doran after he was informed by his staff. Dan bombarded me with questions and pressure to stay, after an hour he gave up and my check was cut. My point was that the presented material did not have a valuable tool to get and find more Gold Nuggets. It appears to me that most attendees at the events never asked for a refund as for them it is normal to pay for college education with no refund for absence when unable to switch to or attend a different class. As born and raised overseas, I have a different mindset. For example, Germans can attend university classes for free, a culture difference.

Besides the hundreds attending all kind of Real Estate Education Classes, and many of these attendees naming a town in SW-Florida as their home turf and money available at every corner, my mind was wondering why just a few became active in the market. What happened to the rest who spend 5 digit amounts on workshops and home study courses? The same happened in my workshops, just a few took action.

Invited to a workshop as Guest speaker, I spoke with the event staff about their experience of action taking, They told me less than 50% of the attendees take further action to implement the course material and invest in Real Estate long- or short term. Even people who spend more money on coaching produce more than 40% dropouts.

What happens to their dreams? Their idea to create an extra income or to get out of the typical 9-5 rat race?

From my perspective all Real Estate Investment Gurus give you a big toolbox of different opportunities and _their_ proven path to success in Real Estate. But what is the missing link, what does make the difference?

Maybe a starting point to find an answer is this quote from "The Little Prince":

"If you want to build a ship, don't drum up people to collect wood and don't assign them tasks and work, but rather teach them to long for the endless immensity of the sea." - Antoine de Saint-Exupery

It appears to me that most of the time there was no inspiration how to reach for the stars, no guideline how to transform DIRT into GOLD.

Now a bigger question: ..... how transform a dream into a burning desire inside yourself?

Do you have to find a secret book of an Alchemist to create GOLD?

Another quote has a clue:

"If you think you can do a thing or think you can't do a thing, you're right." Henry Ford

What does it mean? It is simple: YOU!

Your thoughts are creating your inside world, your dreams, your hopes. Nobody but YOU. You are the creator of your actions.

You started your search for financial freedom with the idea of attending a Real Estate Workshop. But are you really ready and able to transform DIRT to GOLD by just attending and listing ....?

Have you already decided that you are ready for prosperity before you signed up for a class? Do you have the burning desire to have the financial freedom?

Stop here and ask yourself... what are you thinking and speaking about around the topic of finances? What are the discussions you are having with yourself and others about the state of the economy, the Real Estate market, your business, money, and your own financial situation?

Do you see it difficult? See above and I confirm, you are right.

Recognize that positive thoughts and conversations are going to help you to have the abundance of money that you want in your life. Changing your thoughts will change your life.

Why? Because you get what you believe, expect, feel, and focus on. Create a new "idea" for you to focus on that will help you grow your financial prosperity.

Every day, take some time to relax, calm your mind and feel how grateful you are for what you have... family, friends, food, AC, clean water, hot shower, fresh coffee, etc.

Relaxed say your new idea loud in front of a mirror, write it down, and know in every moment that it is true!

You add to your idea this sentences:

I am so grateful that I am a magnet for money. I am wealthy now. I create prosperity of every kind all around me. I am a very successful investor. I have the ability to create GOLD out of DIRT. I think BIG, and then allow myself to accept even more good from this amazing life which I create. Wherever it is that I work, I am deeply appreciated and well compensated. I have unlimited choices, and I see and act on the magnificent opportunities that are everywhere. Today is a delightful sunny day! Money comes to me in expected and unexpected ways. I delight in the financial freedom that is a constant in my life. I radiate success, and prosper wherever I turn.

If you prefer to work with questions, you can change the sentences to questions by using "WHY":

Why am I able to create prosperity of every kind all around me? Why does money comes to me in expected and unexpected ways?

By the way, you can record it on your smartphone as memo and listen to it in your car or other places several times a day.

"Don't say, 'If I could, I would.' Say, 'If I can, I will.'"- Jim Rohn

Improving your financial situation takes action, and the actions are going to be the most effective when you have the right mindset with a burning desire. Inspired action is action with intent, focus, and knowing that the effort that you are putting forth will produce much better results. In other words, you must expect that the actions you take are going to produce the results you want. Opportunities present themselves and inspiration flows to you when your mind is very calm and focused. At times like these, you just "know" what to do next. Our intuition is heightened and feeling good give you motivation to move forward, doing what needs to get done.

A calm mindset is the key to your success. Always remember, you create what you want when you feel good, so it is necessary to have a positive attitude around money. Money is no evil, money is your best friend. Feeling good consistently, with an underlying solid foundation of happiness, expands your creativity, focus, and ability to engage with others in a way that gets you the results that you want.

Here are some steps to help you move your life to financial abundance and create GOLD NUGGETS in Real Estate:

1. Take advantage of the economy by having an abundant mindset (regardless of the state of the economy.) History has shown us repeatedly that there are always individuals and companies that find a way to thrive under any circumstance. So, put your mind and heart in the right space and begin again to dream BIG! There are no limits! Create your GOLD NUGGETS!

2. Decide what you want and write it down. Be specific, and focus on it with deep faith. Feel the joy as you think about having what you want as though you already have it. When it comes to money, a Harvard study has proven that you'll be 1000% more successful when you write down your financial goal.

3. Create a snapshot of the desired outcome in your mind and see it often throughout your day. We think in pictures so if you have a photo of what you want (my family, my dream house, my car, my plane, my boot), put a picture on your phone or on your refrigerator and glance at it often. Be absolute sure to feel how good it feels to have it as though you already do.

4. 😎 Focus every day on the many things you already have in your life to be thankful for. This will cause an "upward spiral" of even more things to be thankful for. When you learn to move through your day with a feeling of love and gratitude, for everyone and everything, you will find yourself having more fun than ever.

5. 😄 Never ever underestimate the importance of having fun! Focus on having fun in all your activities. Fun makes you feel good, so you can create what you want more quickly. Laugh more, it is the cheapest medicine on earth for everything.

6. 🖑 List the actions you can take right now, with the information you have at hand. Get started NOW! Thoughts and words are powerful, but actions create the momentum by which your financial situation or business will grow and improve.

This inspired focused action.... will always get you the results you want. This is the secret formula to change DIRT into GOLD NUGGETS.

Whatever you focus on is what you will get more of. When you are focusing on physical, mental, emotional, or spiritual well-being... that is what you will create. You have an incredible power in you to create your life... moment by moment... exactly the way you want it to be. You can shift to what you want by first focusing on the outcome visually, then **feeling** the joy of having it in your life. This requires that you believe it is possible.

But, is simply "believing" enough to create what you desire?

Believing is a good start, but we have all experienced varying degrees of belief. Which says that perhaps we really don't quite believe it yet at all? The truth is that, in order to create what you want, you need to go beyond belief.

There is a fine line between believing and knowing which makes all the difference in you creating the life that you want. "Belief" itself isn't enough. "Believing" is realizing your potential to create something. You may believe that you can create amazing relationships, have more houses with passive income, more money, or better health.

But, you will only do it when you KNOW that you can. You must KNOW it. "Knowing" is faith of an absolute certainty. "Knowing" means that what you want is already "there and happening" in your mind. It is beyond hoping, and it is evidenced by your behavior. You are preparing with the surety of it happening.

> **"It is a gut-level clarity, a total certainty, a complete acceptance as reality of something"**
>
> **Conversations with God, Book 1, Neale Donald Walsch**

So, how do you put this into practice?

In order to create that state of "knowing," you must give thanks in advance for what it is that you want... as if you already have it. Remember, it is been proven in studies that your mind does not know the difference between your current reality and that which you place in your imagination. It just knows what you tell it for example to yourself in the mirror, When you feel really, really good consistently in every moment, and you practice visualizing your desire, you will see it in your reality, in your daily life. Place your effort and time to immerse your mind in whatever you want with gratitude and imagination. Put your complete and total focus on anticipating what you really want. Imagine whatever it is that you truly desire and see and feel the wonderful outcome of your choice, your creation! Have a burning desire!

And remember, your life is like a movie. And do not forget you are the director. You have the amazing ability to create an incredible, awesome movie script, each and every day. You are unique, original, brilliant and outstanding, no one else is like you, you are one of a kind human. So, you want to be sure you create something exciting for yourself today, something that lives up to the standard of the oh-so-powerful YOU that you truly are! Something wonderful, joyful and fun... something that makes you happy now. You live your life one frame at a time, within the movie called "Today." It is entirely up to you how much love, gratitude, and fun you pour into each experience you create to get your desired outcome. And how much dirt you turn into Gold Nuggets. There is no one else to stop you from being a successful Real Estate Investor but YOU.

When someone's statement about the difficulties of having success in Real Estate starts fear of success inside you and you are afraid to fly

REMEMBER fact proves:

Bumblebees can't fly

> Aerodynamically, the bumble bee shouldn't be able to fly, but the bumble bee doesn't know it so it goes on flying anyway
>
> Mary Kay Ash

You're never given a dream without also being given the power to make it true.

At the end two quotes from Richard Bach's Book **Jonathan Livingston Seagull:**

"To fly as fast as thought, to anywhere that is, you must begin by knowing that you have already arrived."

"Break the chains of your thought, and you break the chains of your body, too"

I am happy and grateful to be in Real Estate and live in Florida with all the opportunities, the up and downs, the change of learning. Now I want to give back some of my knowledge gained through experience, research and time. In gratitude for buying this book I offer all readers as a little present the "Quiet Title Workbook" from the above-named workshop. Just send an email to KUK999FL@aol.com - Subject: BOOK - Thank you.

The successful adventure would not be possible without the support in all areas of life, family and business of my wonderful friend, outstanding partner and lovely wife Angie, she is master of office & file organization, bookkeeping and property management, I am blessed to have her walking with me hand in hand through the winds of change.

The limitations of your thoughts are the limits of your acting

---

"The key to success is to focus our conscious mind on things we desire not things we fear."

— Brian Tracy

So don't forget: **BELIEVE IN YOU AND YOUR DREAMS**

Happy and successful investing

AT HOME WITH
DIVERSITY℠

Dr. Klaus U Kattkus
Lic. Real Estate Broker
Dr.Klaus Realty & Investments
Dr.Klaus ER Education & Research

www.drsantaklaus.com
At Home With Diversity Certificate
Chain of Title Research Specialist
www.TheDentMirror.com

WKDW - 97.5 FM
Real Community Radio

**Host and Producer of the Show
"Die Deutschstunde",
WKDW North Port Community Radio 97.5 FM,
German Musik every Sunday 1:00 to 3:00 pm,
online: www.kdwradio.com**

BIO OF DR. KLAUS

ORN AND RAISED in Minden, Germany he immi-grated to USA with his wife and youngest son in 1999 and settled in Florida after a success-ful career in the Restaurant and Baking Industry.

In his spare time in Germany he was a Volunteer Firefighter and an actor on an open-air stage. Interested in alternative healing methods and Quantum Physics and thinking outside the box he became a REIKI-Master and Instructor of Work-shops "Power of Mind - your thoughts create your world". Also invested into himself and attended Seminars conducted by the SILVA MIND Method and the Vera Birkenbihl Method in Ger-many & Austria.

In Florida he learned quickly that the business world is differ-ent, American Football is different to English Football or Ger-man Fussball and Kindergarten has a different meaning as he was a participant and student of the differences in the American and German cultures.

In 2000 he decided to start a new profession in Real Estate, became a Realtor and in 2002 he meet the Real Estate Gurus Ron LeGrand and Lou Brown to learn about Real Estate Investing.

After attending some of these Real Estate Seminars he saw a big opportunity in Land and sold hundreds of Lots in Lee County as Realtor and / or Investor.

Always hungry for more education to fill the buffet of opportunities he attended multiple motivational seminars conducted by Marshall Sylver, Hans Peter Zimmermann, Psych-K Instructor Betty Perry, Silva Mind Lector Ken Cosca, Theta Healing Presenter Vianna Stibal, Amanda Divine and of course Real Estate boot camps by my friend Lou Brown (yeah baby!), Russ Whitney, Ron LeGrand, Kris Krischner, Robyn Thompson and others.

During the crisis he developed a Quiet Title Workshop after struggling to get short sales approved and saw the special warranty deeds popping up. The preparation for the workshop needed in deep research of the internet, County and Court Records and reading the documents in thousands of hours in hundreds of nights.

This insight gives him the opportunity to educate customers and members of the FGCREIA of issues in the Chain of Title of a Property before closing on a deal.

CHAPTER 8
ELITE REAL ESTATE PROFESSIONAL CPA RICK DONNER

PRECIOUS TIME BY the hour. Flat pricing is difficult because some people bring in messes and it makes it difficult to quote a flat fee. Others have no clue about entities and how to be organized. Over time I've developed my basic list of tips to save HUGE amounts of money with your CPA. I hope you will use these cost-saving ideas and be better prepared for your CPA meetings. These tips will save you time and money once you are organized to do them. I want you to have tremendous success in your real estate investing career. Don't be bogged down in the details – go make money. Leave the details to us CPAs.

Who am I?

Real Estate Investing is one if not the easiest way to accumulate wealth over time. I was single until I met my wife Lisa in about 2000. We were married in 2002 when I was 48. I married "up" and Lisa is my complement. You see God made me an accountant, a Thinker Brain, and Lisa thinks like a reptile. She is a quick, fast thinking, and a very savvy woman that everyone loves. She is a born leader. As it turns out we are both entrepreneurs. She is always on the cutting edge with new ideas and opportunities moving forward and I am a strong sounding board as I track our numbers.

Over time Lisa and I have grown efficient in tracking our numerous companies' activities. We don't just do real estate... we live real estate investing. I get jazzed by real estate investing and living it. We are not realtors as many times we've seen investors make more money than the realtors who do a lot of the work. For us, real estate has added to our other streams of income and I must say it has created a fair amount of our savings and cash flow. Typically we keep multi-unit properties for long-term wealth and cash flow and we flip houses for chunks of cash. We've raised private money, purchased and sold commercial property, we've done notes – gotten discounts on notes, as well as foreclosed on them.

Lisa and I have attended many different Guru real estate seminars and traveled all over the country attending the seminars. For us many times these are our vacations. We were mentors for one of the national real estate Gurus for 5 years, mentoring US as well as Canadian and Australian students. We continue to mentor our own students today. Because I do, and have experienced what we as investors do, I have developed strategic, money saving, tips that I teach people and consult about on how to protect themselves and save money working with their CPA. I'd like to share some of those strategic, money-saving ideas with you here. First let's review a little entity structuring and why. Let's get started!!!

Entities of Choice

This is one of the most crucial things you need to know, and do. In real estate investing as in any business you should operate in an entity. I recommend highly the LLC. There are also corporations and trusts to name a couple. I am all about saving you money on set up and administrative costs if you are new. Suppose you were recently to a real estate investing seminar and you are all set and ready to go do your first deal. By all means get your marketing started and bring in those leads because that is what you will be doing your deals from.

I'm sure you already thought up a name for your business. Check to see that the Business name is not used by doing a name search at your state's "Division of Corporations" website. A state won't license the same name to more than one entity. It should only take a couple days to get your new entity set up. Just as soon as you see it is set up at the state website you go online to irs.gov and apply for a Federal "Employer Identification Number", EIN for your new entity. If you need help we can do this for you.

The most important reason to operate in an entity with an EIN is so that when you are out transacting business you give out your Business Name and EIN. Without an Entity and EIN you'd be giving your social security number out to people and in today's environment of Identity Theft you don't want to do that.

The LLC can be taxed in different ways. A single member LLC, SMLLC, has one owner and in our state of Florida it does not have much asset protection. The SMLLC is taxed as a sole proprietor. If the LLC has more than one owner, otherwise known as members, it is a multi-member LLC and has better asset protection than a SMLLC due to charging order protection. A new multi-member LLC is taxed as a Partnership. Through special election with IRS Form 8832 the LLC can also be taxed as a Corporation and with IRS Form 2553 an S Corporation.

Lastly, I like the LLC because it is an easy entity to set up and administer. The LLC is also flexible in how it is taxed. After you are up and running a while, and in consultation with your CPA, it may make sense to use the Form 8832 to convert your LLC to a Sub S corporation. Under current rules you can only change type of entity once every 5 years. We will learn more about this in "Buckets of Activity".

Buckets of Activity

Lisa and I are really excited about real estate investing and over the years have helped many people achieve success. As real estate mentors we teach that almost any lead can generate a deal if you and the seller come to terms. As your business evolves and you are doing more deals you will see patterns in your business. You may find that you are holding some properties and flipping some properties. You may be holding enough properties and you like managing them so you start a property management business. Maybe you are good at raising money and find that you have an ability to become a loan broker, private lender, or hard money lender. Maybe you purchase, rehab, and flip 10 - 50 properties or more a year. Maybe you become a realtor or real estate broker. There are so many variations of how your business could change and evolve that it is hard to examine all here but let me give you a couple examples and how your LLC taxability may change.

I like to refer to the type of activity as different buckets of activity. One bucket of activity is holding property. Another bucket of activity would include flips and most of the other things you do in real estate investing. It can be subjective until you get to a good size and see the patterns or buckets of activity which can only really be determined by a discussion with a CPA knowledgeable about real estate investing. If you are holding property you will want an LLC for holding property and a separate LLC taxed as an S corporation to run most of the other business activity through.

When Lisa and I started real estate investing our first deal made about $125,000. At the time we were flipping quite a few properties and generated substantial profits. (I wish they all made $125,000 but they didn't.) I determined we needed 2 entities. One LLC we held properties in and the other we elected to be taxed as an S corporation because we were earning substantial "business" income from flipping. With an S Corporation, the nature of your income is changed because of tax election from self-employment income taxation to business income made from a corporation which has no extra 15.3% tax for social security and Medicare. With a couple flips a year you can save money by taxing each as a capital gain type deal and minimize taxes. When you start doing quite a few flip deals a year – and it is very subjective – but, the more deals you are doing, you really are "in business". Once you pass the threshold where you are flipping quite a few properties and you are not taxed as an S corporation you become what's known to the IRS as a "dealer" and if audited they may convert all your earnings to business income and not tax you at capital gain rates but ordinary tax rates PLUS an extra 15.3% tax for social security and Medicare. IRS audits happen a couple years after the books are done and you are penalized on anything the IRS finds wrong for being late.

This is exactly where Lisa and I were. We decided to do our flips through the S corporation to save on the extra 15.3% social security and Medicare tax. However, when you have an S Corporation operating a business the owners need to take a reasonable salary from the company that is comparable to the average person in the industry.

Let me give you an example. If you have "net income" after all business expenses of $100,000, and you are not taxed as an S Corporation, the regular income tax rate is about 20% or $20,000. In addition you are also taxed the extra 15.3% for social security and Medicare, an additional $15,300 for a total tax of $35,300 out of your $100,000. That is choking for an entrepreneur who needs money to operate their business plus live.

Conversely, with an S corporation, in the same example and you make the same $100,000, the income tax remains the same $20,000. However rather than pay the extra 15.3% for social security and Medicare on the whole $100,000 you pay a reasonable salary to the owner equal to the average in the industry. I don't know if there is an average salary for a real estate investor but let's say you pay yourself a salary of $2,500 a month for a total of $30,000 for the year. Your S corporation will issue you a W2 for $30,000 at the end of the year. By having your S corporation pay you a salary of $30,000 you pay the extra 15.3% on only $30,000 of the $100,000 or $4,590 not the full $15,300 thereby saving you $10,710 in extra tax. In the end the $100,000 is still yours, we just split it in to a W2 for $30,000 and the S corporation distributes to you the $70,000 in distributions taxable at your regular tax bracket.

If you look at a W2 you see there are 3 taxes withheld. Box 2 is income tax based on your tax bracket and how you fill out the W4 you give an employer. Boxes 4 and 6 are social security and Medicare and withhold 7.65% out of each paycheck. The 7.65% does not change. The employer matches the 7.65% and pays the 15.3% collected from your 7.65% and their matching to the US Treasury. If you are not an S Corporation you pay both sides for the total of 15.3%.

That was pretty technical but the point is if you are doing a lot of business other than holding real estate you probably want to be taxed as S corporation and pay yourself a salary on a W2. The beauty is that all the $100,000 in the prior example is yours to do with as you please but we just reported part on a W2 and the rest will flow through to you on a K1 form from the S corporation. You will want to talk to your CPA about your situation.

Oops, I almost forgot to tell you about the other LLC. If you are accumulating a portfolio of real estate holdings it is best to hold them in a multi-member LLC with each property being titled in a land trust. The LLC is the beneficial owner of each land trust. The multi-member holding LLC will be taxed as a partnership. With the multi-member LLC you will have charging order, asset protection and with the land trust, if done properly, it will be difficult for the public and tenants to know who the property owner is. When we are at any of our properties we always tell the tenant we are with the management company.

Orderly and Cost-Saving Accounting Records

As a CPA I've sat across the desk from many people and can assess your story in about 30 minutes. I can then direct how you should be structured and what type of entity or entities you will need. There will be questions back and forth and a proper discussion should be why you do certain things in certain ways. You need to understand the Big picture. Your CPA can handle the details. Once you understand the Big picture we may take in data and select names for your LLCs and touch on how to keep records. Once we have come to an understanding and agree to work together you can save money with your accounting fees by being time-efficient for your CPA. Come to all meetings prepared and be on time. Write legibly. You want to make the CPA firm's job as easy as possible. Be considerate of the CPA's time as most bill you for their time "invested" in working for you. That is the CPA business model. Let's get started on some ways to be most efficient for your CPA.

Have a Business bank account, debit card, and 1 credit card for each entity. As soon as we've established your entity you need to open your bank account. You will make a Capital Contribution deposit to start your business. From there all expenses should be paid by check or debit card. If you need more money deposit another capital contribution. In addition we recommend using 1 credit card for all expenses that can't be paid with the debit card or by check. The credit card is a revolving line of credit that you charge bills on and pay on monthly. Only business expenses should be paid with this credit card. If you are ever audited by the IRS and you have a mixture of personal and business items charged the IRS can disallow all the credit card interest deduction because there is to be "no mixed use" of business and personal expenses charged on the card.

With 1 bank account with a debit card and 1 credit card, all your transactions are in a couple easy to find places. We highly recommend QuickBooks as they have desktop versions of the software and QuickBooks Online, QBO, you can sub-scribe to. You can format either to import your transactions from the bank and credit card to the QuickBooks. If you have the desktop version of QuickBooks you can e-mail an Accoun-tant's copy to your CPA where they can make adjustments to it and export entries back to you. With QBO you invite your CPA to access your QBO books through an online feature.

To save money on accounting fees only pay business expenses through the business accounts. If you pay personal bills such as personal grocery bills, utilities and any other items this increases the amount of work for the CPA firm. Do not co-min-gle business and personal expenses.

Rather than track all your car expenses and buy or title your vehicle in the business many times we have clients keep a mileage log of all their business activity. In an IRS audit you will be asked for mileage logs of the vehicles to substanti-ate the business expenses. The ratio of personal to business miles is taken times the total vehicle expense and that is the write-off. Any personal percentage is disallowed. Remember to include mileage for trips to the post office, CPA, attorney, and client meetings, searching for office supplies, etc. even if you don't buy anything. Today there are many Apps that can help you track your mileage.

One task you will want to do is gather all your costs prior to setting up your entity that were not paid through the entity bank account. These will be start-up costs and can include seminars, travel, education, the cost of the entity, CPA fees, attorney fees, mileage, office, and the list goes on. Your CPA should give you another Capital Contribution credit for these costs.

Independent Contractor vs Employee is one of the biggest hot-topic, client compliance, issues for CPAs and a huge tar-get area of the IRS. Many entrepreneurs and business owners don't want to do the hassles of payroll filings or pay their share of the SS and Medicare matching as we discussed above so they think they can just issue IRS Form 1099MISC to everyone that works for them. I'm sorry to say you can't do that but unfortunately some of you will no matter how much we beg you not to. It is too much to explain here but for simplicity sake the more you control what and when the person does for you and especially if the person is not in the business of doing the services for others they are probably an employee and should be paid through payroll and issued a W2.

You should have all people that work for you fill out IRS Form W9. Independent contractors are issued IRS form 1099MISC if you pay them over $600 in a year. Form 1099MISC is due to the independent contractor by January 31 each year and a copy sent to the IRS so the IRS can match what the Independent Contractor files to what you said they were paid. By the end of December total up all payments you made to your Independent Contractors and give these to your CPA firm with the W9s in early January so they can have them ready for you. Make sure the W9s are very legible because you will be scrambling to get the correct information if not.

I recommend that everyone in business carry a stack of W9s in their briefcase. The best time to have an independent Contractor fill out a W9 is when you hand them their first check. Once again make sure you can read the writing on the W9.

On all business tax returns there is a question: "Did the business pay anyone that should have gotten a 1099?" This forces us as income-tax preparers to let the IRS know you were to issue 1099s. You could be in trouble with the IRS if you did not issue the 1099s.

Specific Documents to Give your CPA

There are a few items you will want your CPA to have. These are a good start on the list.

- <u>Your best contact</u> information including cell telephone number and e-mail.

- <u>Corporate documents</u> including Articles of Incorporation, or, Articles of Organization, and Bylaws.

- <u>EIN letter from IRS</u>. When you have set up an entity and applied for an EIN from the IRS the IRS will issue a letter to the entity owner saying how you are taxed as well as any filing dates and any other tax filings you may be liable for related to that EIN.

- <u>W9s</u> for Independent Contractors as Explained above.

- If you have prepared <u>payroll copies</u> of your quarterly reports and year-end W2s issued and especially the W2(s) to the owner(s).

- <u>Password to your QBO</u>, or, if desktop QuickBooks, year of QuickBooks, and password.

- <u>Settlement statements</u> for purchases and sales of properties.

- Once you have established a relationship with a CPA they usually send you a <u>tax organizer</u> at the beginning of each year that is a checklist of items potentially needed for the preparation of your taxes.

Summary

In closing I want to say that I hope you will use these cost-saving ideas and be better prepared for your CPA meetings. These tips will save you time and money once you are organized to do them. Lisa and I want you to have tremendous success in your real estate investing careers. Don't be bogged down in the details – go make money. Leave the details to us CPAs. I am afraid many don't keep adequate records but if you can follow the simple, strategic, cost-saving ideas above you will be way ahead of your competition. Your CPA can fill in the Gaps.

<u>Lisa and I have attended many boot camps and seminars</u> on all facets of real estate investing and spent tens of thousands of dollars doing so <u>and it was well worth it</u>. We continue attending multiple trainings and boot camps each year to stay on the cutting edge of techniques and market opportunities

We've personally done, and coached and taught, on many aspects of real estate investing including deal analysis, buying and selling single family and multi-family, negotiating, commercial property, and other aspects of this business. This is my 5th book. The first book Lisa and I co-authored with a National Real Estate Guru, the 2nd we wrote our own book on real estate investing, the 3rd and 4th books we co-authored with a group of like-minded Business Leaders and wrote about Business Leadership. ***All 4 of our prior books were #1 Best Selling Amazon books.*** We love this business and enjoy sharing it with others. Because I am a real estate investor and know what you do I have simplified the process, the accounting, and tax implications in our own businesses. Most of all it has helped me know how to help you the most – because I do it for myself. Simply follow the guidelines above and you will be miles ahead of others around you.

If you have questions or need advice do not hesitate to contact us. My website at www.donnercpa.com has a free tax, bookkeeping and accounting newsletter you can subscribe to. My office line is 239.541.9494.

If you call and mention this book, and chapter, we will send you one of our 4, #1 Amazon Best Selling Books.

Lisa and I wish you the best in all your endeavors.

Rick Donner, CPA
Real estate CPA, coach and mentor

RICK DONNER, CPA BIO:

RICK DONNER CPA is from northwest PA and always liked and excelled in math and today is a CPA. Rick's first accounting position was at a CPA firm that had a concentration in ranch and grove accounting, and, many small to medium-sized businesses of all kinds.

Today Rick owns and manages Donner & Company, CPA, PA and is found on the web at www.donnercpa.com. Rick has a unique process where he analyzes the clients' objectives and assesses their current position and then helps the client meet their projected goals. At Donner & Company CPA Rick helps clients "Save Taxes" and provides tax, accounting, consulting, and QuickBooks services to small to medium-sized businesses, their owners, and other high net-worth individuals.

In Rick's spare time he invests in real estate. He and his wife Lisa like to travel and look at real estate everywhere they go – even internationally. Rick and Lisa personally buy and sell houses, coach and mentor others on how to buy and sell houses without using their money or credit and using other creative buying and selling strategies, have done commercial, private money, apartments and a host of other real estate strategies. They continue to do these strategies today.

Rick always says "Every deal is different. When you have a whole arsenal of real estate strategies and tools at your disposal that others don't know, we take down deals that others pass up. Not all strategies work on every deal. If you are in real estate and need a CPA you really need a CPA that is doing deals of all kinds and understands the tax strategies. The only way you know something the best is to be doing it yourself." If you need a business CPA that knows business and real estate – Rick Donner CPA is your guy. Rick challenges you to Google him and see all the reviews he has. Here are a couple of the Google (out of all 28 – 5 star) reviews:

Jason A: Tax prep and Planning

"I wanted a professional CPA to prepare my taxes. I called around and some CPAs wanted outrages prices or wouldn't bother to follow up with me. I knew Rick was the right guy when he was giving me advice even before I agreed to be his client. He just seems like a great guy who likes to help people."

Juan C: Dentist

"Rick is an experienced CPA and hardworking. I had some issues on a previous TAX returns and I was working with 2 other CPAs for 6 over months and had many issues getting things done when I went to see Rick he had everything taken care of accurately within 2 weeks. I highly recommend Rick."

Mark I: Real Estate Investor

"I am lucky to have found Donner & Company CPA and consider them to be an integral part of my business and a true partner. I've gone through 5 CPA firms before finding Donner & Company CPA. The other CPA companies simply took my tax materials, farmed them out to entry-level accountants, and overcharged me with no justification. In addition, I always found errors in their work that caused me numerous revisions and additional costs. My experience with Donner & Company CPA is the exact opposite! The owner, Rick Donner, spent a significant amount time learning my business and personal tax requirements. In addition, he performed a historical review of my taxes, found all the issues, and corrected them accordingly.

I would recommend anyone looking for a CPA, that is a true partner and understands tax regulations, to contact Donner and & Company CPA. I'm happy I did!"

Rick Donner CPA can be found on the web at www.donner-cpa.com or reached by telephone at 239.541.9494.

CHAPTER 9
ELITE REAL ESTATE PROFESSIONAL MOE MATHEWS

**Better, More, Greater:
Applying Marine Corp Principles
to Create a Fresh Start
Approach to Investing**

NO DOUBT YOU'RE wondering what Marine Corp principles could possibly have to do with investing, in particular real estate investing. Well, I'll tell you. Are you ready?

I firmly believe that applying the principles and behaviors I learned from over thirteen years in the Marine Corp has helped me achieve success in investing. And it can help you as well. You could apply these same principles to any area of business, but I'm going to show you how you can use them to be successful at investing, specifically real estate investing. Not because these principles are harder to incorporate into other types of investing, but because real estate is where I found success and I want to share my experience with you.

Over the course of my thirteen-plus years with the Marine Corp, I've held nearly every position possible. I've been a rifleman, mechanic, platoon sergeant, logistics officer, drill instructor, and was selected to the rank of warrant officer by the Secretary of the Navy at the age of twenty-eight. To this day, I am still the youngest person promoted to warrant officer in the history of the Marine Corp.

By the time I retired from the Marine Corp as the chief warrant officer, I was a highly-decorated war veteran. I've pretty much done it all. The same is true with real estate investing. I'm currently the president of my local real estate investors association. I'm also a real estate investor/franchise owner, builder, developer, wholesaler, and philanthropist. I've helped hundreds of folks just like you set up their own real estate investing business. And I believe I can help you as well.

Yet, just like everyone else, I had to start at the bottom. The best advice I've ever gotten while serving in the Marine Corp was to volunteer for everything. When I first got into investing I dabbled in stocks and options, but I never found any success. There are a lot of investors out there floundering in stocks or day trading, affected by the volatility of the market. It took a long time for me to realize there is more than one way to invest. Even after I discovered real estate investing, it wasn't until I applied the principles and behaviors I learned in the Marine Corp that I truly found success.

The Marine Corps taught me to go through it, around it, or over it. If you have an obstacle, you have to find a way to move past it, even if the way isn't clearly visible in the beginning. As members of the Marine Corp, we are all instilled with a can-do attitude. We'll do what needs to be done, even if something isn't in our job description. Moving forward is the only way to achieve mission accomplishment. It's how you move forward, the support team you have in place, and the tools you use that will determine if that mission is a success or not.

Even within real estate investing, there are multiple ways you can be successful, or what I like to call your real estate menu. You can select one item from the menu and see how that method tastes before moving on to the next course. Or you can have the buffet as I did, doing wholesale deals, buy-and-hold deals, fix-and-flips, and cash-on-cash returns. Real estate really allows you to be creative, to slice up each transaction in different ways. I've handled over a thousand transactions in my real estate investing career and not two have been identical.

As a teacher and mentor, I encourage all of my investors to look at each opportunity with a relentless attitude to make it work. Sometimes the challenge is greater, but the payoff is also greater. Taking on those challenging, seemingly-impossible deals is the only way to learn and practice your trade. You can't learn anything new by doing transactions that are exactly the same, day in and day out. You can't find new ways to increase your profit margins either. And isn't that the whole reason you decided to get into real estate investing to begin with? Use every transaction as an opportunity to learn, to find the gold nuggets that other investors overlook. Remember, a deal is never dead until it has been transferred to someone else.

If there is one message I hope you will take away from this book, it would be to *do it now*. Don't wait to start creating passive income. If you've been hesitating for whatever reason, don't let it stop you from achieving your goals. Now is the time to take that first step, to move forward and I can show you how. Perhaps you want to invest but haven't been able to find the time. Or maybe you like the idea of investing in real estate, but the process seems too challenging or cumbersome. Whatever obstacle is in your path, I can help you find ways to go over it, around it, or through it.

I hope to use my experience as a training tool, to help walk you through the process so you can find out what works best for you and your investing goals. After going through my training, many of my investors feel comfortable enough to take on every step of the process themselves, while others prefer to have a management company like mine, Fresh Start Property Solutions, handle all of the details. Whichever method they choose, the process is understandable and exciting for them, and I know it can be for you as well.

A lot of investors don't have the knowledge or capability to *buy it right*, because they are dependent on someone else's experience or knowledge. Many folks are too willing to take someone else's opinion as fact instead of doing research on their own. As an investor, you need to take control of each deal and understand what's there. This is *your* cash flow stream we're talking about after all. It's important to have the willingness to go out and find answers, to get second opinions. If a doctor told you that you had cancer, wouldn't you get a second opinion? So, why don't we, as investors, get second opinions when it comes to doing deals?

While it's true that beginning investors often don't know what they don't know, the difference between the successes and the failures is knowledge. Go out and talk to somebody. If you never ask, you will never get an answer.

As you read through this book, I will show you how to network, how to market to your target audience, and the most important piece—to set goals. I will cover all of the steps in the real estate investing process, from documentation and negotiations to deal structure and management. I will also show you how I applied the principles I learned in the Marine Corp to get to where I am today with fifteen local franchises and five others nationwide. So, are you ready? Let's get started.

Clear Sight Alignment and Sight Picture

The first step toward achieving success, in investing or any aspect of life, really should be setting goals. After getting into real estate investing, one of the things I eventually noticed was that the folks who had goals were more successful than those who didn't. It might seem simple enough. Pretty much everyone sets goals at the start of the New Year, right? However, don't move onto the next chapter just yet. There is more to goal-setting than simply thinking one up.

Oftentimes, folks tend to set their sights too broad or too far, instead of narrowing their goal down and focusing on what's really important. This was the problem I had when I first got into real estate investing. Because I didn't have proper goals, I spent a lot of my time putting out fires. I didn't know where I was headed, so I had no roadmap. Without a destination, you can't chart a path to get there. I knew I wanted to get involved with investing, but I just ended up dabbling in all kinds of trades with no real direction. I would often joke that I was a jack of all trades, but a master of none. For me, it created a lot of wasted time, energy, and money.

In the beginning, I had attended a lot of trainings, and studied a lot of books. However, the problem was I never applied what I learned because I wasn't listening to what was most important to me at the time. I ended up spending three years doing things I didn't need to do. I wasted money and time on marketing and advertising, and on developing a real estate investing business without really having a goal or a reason why I was doing what I was doing.

I'm an on the job training kind of guy. So, when things weren't working out, I started asking other investors I met what worked for them and what didn't. For the things that went wrong, I asked them what they would do to change it. That was how I learned about the importance of setting goals. I noticed a pattern between the investors who didn't have goals and how they were performing.

Networking, talking to other folks in your industry or field, can help you see where you're headed and what you don't want to do. But I will get into that in the next chapter. The first step, however, is setting a goal and getting it down on paper. While writing out your goals may seem unimportant—your goals can change after all—getting your goals down on paper helps you stay focused.

In the Marine Corp, I learned how to be a marksman. All Marines are marksmen. In order to sight a target, to focus on our goal, we had to have clear sight alignment and sight picture. Basically, that means that we had to be able to see our target clearly or none of our shots would hit. If the target was too far away, we needed to adjust the scope and account for wind speed and direction.

Putting your goals on paper doesn't set them in stone. They can change, and they should change, especially if you surpass them or decide they are no longer important. Yet, you have got to have a starting point. Without a set destination, you are more likely to take detours. The same is true for setting goals. You have to put it on paper or you are more likely to forget your goal, to lose sight of your target. It has to be on paper.

The best way I've found to make sure to get my goals down on paper, and to really zero in on my target, is to do the following exercise. This exercise really helped me to free-form my goal-searching sessions. After I did this exercise for the first time and realized how well it worked, I started doing it quarterly. And now, I'm doing this same exercise with the folks I'm mentoring, and the same result is happening. Whether it's on the phone or live and in person, this exercise works to help people narrow down their goals to what is truly important and to get their goals on paper, and it can work for you, too. I've done this exercise many different ways and with many different people, yet I haven't had it fail once.

Exercise (I recommend repeating the following steps at least quarterly.)

All you need to perform this exercise is five minutes, paper and a pen or pencil, and a quiet place. My favorite time to do this exercise is early in the morning on a Sunday. After you've had the whole weekend to deal with the good and the bad, you can take just five minutes and really focus on everything you want, and I mean everything. You don't have to just focus on business or your investment ventures. Use these five minutes to free-form in writing anything and everything you want.

Start by asking yourself, *what do you want*? I record myself asking this question over and over again for five minutes, changing the tonality and volume of my voice. Then I play it back and write down everything that comes to my mind while I listen to my voice. Remember, this is between you and yourself. No one else will see what you write. Playback your recording while you write down on sheets and sheets of paper, front and back, everything that you want. It might not seem that hard, but it's arduous. However, I bet that if anyone does this exercise they will find it eye-opening.

Even if you think you've written everything down, continue free-forming, without any interruptions, for the full five minutes. The amount of time you do this exercise is extremely important, because it's only after the first minute that you start to really get down to what is most important to you personally, in all aspects of life. You will start to pinpoint certain areas in business, health, life, family, and relationships. Your ideas will start forming groups and circling back around to certain things. The things that are most important to you will repeat over and over.

This is where the Marine Corp principle of having clear sight alignment and sight picture really comes into play. If I'm truly zeroing in on my target, then all my shots are landing in a certain group. They are clustered together. By doing this exercise for the full five minutes, you start to get laser-focused and zeroed in on what you want on every section of life. All of this free-forming funnels down into what is really important to you and what you can accomplish.

Once the five minutes is up, review everything you wrote down. The vague stuff on your paper is your more long-term goals, while the specific things, or zeroed-in stuff, is your short-term goals. By doing this exercise repeatedly, I have been able to get my goals zeroed down to where I know exactly what my current vision is. My goal isn't just to be successful in real estate investing. In addition to setting a specific annual income I want to reach, my goal is also to help a hundred-thousand service members, particularly Marines, get into executive positions and become entrepreneurs, and I want to help one million people get a fresh start, because everybody deserves one.

Most folks seem to think you can have short-term goals without setting long-term goals, and vice versa, but I truly believe you can't achieve one without the other. Long- and short-term goals really do go hand in hand. If you only set short-term goals, you are losing sight of your target downrange, of your destination. And if you have long-term goals without setting short-term goals, you have a destination but no roadmap of how to get there.

I encourage the investors I mentor to break down their goals, not just into long- and short-term, but into timelines of ten years, five years, three years, one year, ninety-days and weekly goals. If the content is not there to achieve our long-term goals, then we get there, we can build it up by focusing on short-term goals. If you did the exercise for the full five minutes then getting your short- and long-term goals from your free-form writing should just be a matter of prioritizing. The longer you free-form, the more laser-focused your shots downrange will become, the more specific your goals will be.

By prioritizing and organizing your goals, you will create the true essence of what is most important to you right now and what you need to be focused on to get you there. For example, if my ninety-day goal is to close a set number of deals, what do my weekly goals need to be to get me to that ninety-day goal? How many phone calls or property tours do I need to schedule each week? What kinds of marketing campaigns should I focus on, or how many doors do I need to knock on? Weekly goals might be as simple as calling a certain company, or creating an email marketing campaign. It can be whatever it takes to get the phone to ring. Remember, you have to start the journey to your goal somewhere and that is what short-term or weekly goals are all about.

I'm all about multitasking. I like to do multiple things at once that help me accomplish multiple goals. I want to accomplish the most number of things in the shortest amount of time, but I also want it to be fun. People often overlook that piece, but when you think about it, if a task isn't fun, you're more reluctant to get it done. So, when I set my short-term goals, I look for ways I can make it fun. I look for ways I can accomplish multiple goals at once. Not just business goals, but health or family goals as well. For example, I might take a conference call while walking on my treadmill. Ask yourself how you can do more than one thing at once.

Setting short-term goals also ensure that your goals, both long- and short-term are measurable. How will you know if you're headed in the right direction if you don't have a way to measure how far you've gone? By setting weekly goals, you automatically have a way to measure your progress toward your ninety-day goal. In my earlier example of having a ninety-day goal of closing a set number of deals, I will automatically know how far I've gotten toward that goal each week when I reconcile my accomplishments.

For my ninety-day goal, I know I have to do 40 percent in the first thirty days to ensure I'm on track to achieving my goal. So, by working backwards, I can figure out how much of that I have to do in the first week. From there, you can break it down even further into items that are most important to do today. Breaking your ninety-day goal down into weekly accomplishments turns into measurements you can use to assess your progress. It also helps you see where you might be lacking. How close did you get to your ninety-day goal? What can you change for the coming week to get closer?

The bottom line is that it's got to be fun and you've got to win. It's good for the ego to win. When you beat yourself up about what you didn't accomplish or the things you didn't do as well as you could have, then all you're focusing on is the negative. Celebrating and acknowledging accomplishments is just as important as actually accomplishing them.

While breaking down your goals into daily and weekly tasks will help you measure and reach your goals, it can be arduous to keep track of everything. This is why utilizing technology is so important. We are lucky enough to live in an age where we can automate nearly any task. We can write digital notes and share them with anyone in an instant. You can prioritize your notes, creating a workflow of what you have to get done. There are tons of applications and tools available to help you organize and plan the tasks that need to be accomplished. One of the tools and applications I've found useful is *Plannerpad.com*. Other tools include *Evernote*, *Notes* for Apple devices, and *Notepad* for Windows. When it comes to achieving your goals, you use everything you have within your means. Whatever kind of text application you have on your cell phone, utilize it to jot things down, to keep track of ideas and lists of things to do. I even use my cell phone to take pictures of receipts so I can upload the information directly into my accounting software. Not only does it save time, it reduces the amount of paperwork I have to deal with. You also don't have to go searching very far to find everything that you need when you have these tools at your fingertips.

There are other applications that are especially useful for real estate investors, such as sketching apps like *Skitch*. These applications allow you to create arrows and comments right on photos so you can point out issues with a property to potential clients. Another application, *Whiteboard* lets you free-form your notes and share them with anyone. Its free-style format allows for more creativity. *Basecamp, Workflowy,* and *If at then this* are other tools I use regularly. I'm a firm believer in automation. Anything you can use which saves you time is a valuable tool to have in your arsenal.

One of my favorite tools isn't even electronic, but it's one of the best ways I've found to help me organize my day. It's called a 4-person calendar book. The planner has four columns for each day, designed to log the schedule of four different people. However, I use the different columns to organize my days. The first column is my appointments, meetings or conference calls, things I absolutely have to be present for. The second column is for the things I can and need to get done within gaps of time between appointments. The third column is for brainstorming, the things I want to get done or the items that come up during the day, which I will do at my earliest convenience, such as returning phone calls. The fourth column is for distractions, things that come up during the day which I need to reply to. Having that fourth column is great because it eliminates the need for post-it notes and message slips. It allows me to resolve and fix things throughout my day without losing track of anything. This planner becomes your journal, a record of the progress you've made toward your goal.

The Marine Corp taught me to have a vision, a mission, and a goal, and it was only by applying that principle to my real estate ventures that I finally started to see progress. It doesn't matter how small or big you think your goal is. By doing the exercise I described in this chapter, you will be able to narrow your goal down into measurable weekly accomplishments. It will also get your goals down on paper. It is much easier to hold yourself accountable to your goals when you have them documented.

Once you have your goals set, you can take your first actionable step toward achieving those goals by networking, learning, and adding value. I'll tell you more about how to do that in the next chapter. Like many beginning investors, you might be starting at the bottom, but by having a roadmap of where you're headed, you can forge on without the uncertainty so many other investors face. You will be giving yourself a fresh start each and every week.

Volunteer for Everything

Whether you are a seasoned investor or just starting out, one of the biggest things you can do to move toward achieving your goals is to increase your knowledge. Sounds simple, right? Well, it can be; however, many investors tend to go about it the hard way. Often they will spend upwards of twenty- or thirty thousand dollars in training and seminars and are still reluctant to buy their first property.

If they are gaining all of this knowledge about investing from these seminars then what's holding them back? It may be that they don't know how to turn this newfound knowledge into action. I believe there are some things you can only learn by doing, by putting yourself out there in the market.

When I first got into real estate investing, I didn't know what I didn't know. I soon realized that anything I did know wasn't good enough because I wasn't buying right. In other words, if the knowledge I had was sufficient, I should have been buying deals in a way that would allow me to turn a profit, yet I wasn't. I was going through the steps but I wasn't reaping any benefit. I realized that the only way I was going to get the knowledge I needed to get deals and buy them right was to surround myself with people who were already doing it and were successful at it.

Jim Rohn said it best. You have to study Failures & Successes. Study the good and bad in every situation and in people. You don't have to tell them about it, you just have to study it. Get a journal and talk to the people who failed at it. Ask them what they did wrong and what they would do to change it. Talk to the people who were successful at it and ask them how they did it. Take notes and study from that knowledge what you need to do to create your own strategy.

Being a part of a larger collective, working with other investors who were doing deals in the markets I was interested in, was how I learned about real estate investing. I networked with others in investing and learned from their experiences.

Networking is the simplest and easiest way to gain knowledge. You can see where you are headed and what you are up against by talking to and studying the people who have already taken that journey. Nothing is going to come from just reading and going to seminars. At some point, you have to take action. You have to surround yourself with people who are in the positions you want to be in and represent your ideals.

In the Marine Corp, we have a saying. *You have to be a great follower before you can become a great leader.* By networking with folks who are doing what you want to be doing, and following their example, you can learn from their experiences. John Maxwell once said to "surround yourself with those that you want to become. Your net worth is the sum total of your network." While you can learn from the failures of others, those aren't the people you want to surround yourself with. If you are looking up to people who have failed at investing, guess what you are going to get – negativity and failure. However, if you are looking up to people who are successful at it, who get results, then you will be able to reap similar results because they will be sharing their knowledge with you through networking.

Networking will not only increase your knowledge, it can help you build your team as well. For example, let's say you specialize in fix-and-flip properties. Well, your real estate agent might be good enough to be your interior designer. Paying one person to do two tasks is not only more cost effective, it's efficient. I will talk more about building your team in the next chapter. By talking to real estate agents, contractors, investors, lawyers, etc., you will find those people who are willing to give you their honest opinion, connect you with others, and who you feel comfortable working with going forward.

The best way I know of to get out there and start networking is to volunteer for everything. This was probably the best piece of advice I got while I was in the Marine Corp. When you hear the word *volunteer*, you probably think of community service events. While these activities are great networking opportunities, the kind of volunteering I'm referring to is offering to do tasks. It is only through action that you are going to get the most amount of experience, both good and bad.

Action creates results. In the Marine Corp, we say that *practice makes perfect, but perfect practices creates mission accomplishment and make perfect results.* We have to continuously practice what we want to accomplish.

Be immersed in activity. After realizing how much I didn't know about real estate investing, I took the advice of volunteering for everything to heart and started working with investors who were buying properties to renovate and resell. I talked to investors who were buying notes and non-performing mortgages. I went to auctions on the courthouse steps to see how that process worked and to meet investors who were buying at auction. I went to the REA group meetings and investor group meetings to learn what was happening in a particular market.

Through action, through doing deals, I was able to network with realtors, banks, investors, and lawyers and learn from their experience. If you are active in the business, the knowledge will come. You can study and take training courses, but at some point you are going to have to go out and try it for yourself. Some knowledge you can only gain by going out and doing, and that is where networking comes into play.

However, networking isn't just about learning through doing; it's about adding value. You can't go to an investment group meeting and try to sponge all of the knowledge off other investors. You have to approach networking with an attitude of give and take. Ask them what they want then go out and get it. Go find it. For example, if they are looking for properties in a certain market, I would go out and find properties for them. I was not only learning by doing, but I was adding value to the relationship by giving back. John Maxwell said, "People who add value to others do so intentionally. I say that because to add value, leaders must give of themselves, and that rarely occurs by accident."

By asking others what they want to buy, it lets me know what they are truly about, what niche they want to get into and what the current market was thriving on. You don't know what people want until you ask. Having the knowledge of what they wanted helped me figure out why they wanted it as well, and what their niche was. In addition, they learned what I was about, what motivated me and what kind of value I could bring to the table.

A well-known acronym in the Marine Corp is JJ DID TIE BUCKLE, which stands for justice, judgment, dependability, integrity, decisiveness, tact, initiative, endurance, bearing, unselfishness, courage, knowledge, loyalty, and enthusiasm. If you focus all of these traits on whatever it is that you want to accomplish, it will add value back to the person that you are trying to learn from.

Networking can help you build opportunities. For example, by going to auctions, I not only had the opportunity to learn something, I was able to build a buyer's list and exchange business cards with other investors. Joining an investor's association or group is another great way to network. If there isn't a group or association in your area, you might consider creating one. There are a variety of ways you can create your own investment club for free. One way would be to advertise your weekly meeting time and location through *Craigslist*. Even the meeting location can be free. Most public libraries have meeting rooms available, or you can meet in coffee shops or restaurants. Meeting in a public place also provides the opportunity of attracting new members. Just remember to meet often and at the same time each week.

You can also create a landing page, use social media, or create a discussion board online. Not only will an investment group build opportunities and broaden your network, it offers accountability. You are more likely to stick with the goals you set by doing the exercise in Chapter One if you are consistently meeting with others who have similar goals each week. Your group doesn't have to be formal. Just have fun doing it.

As I mentioned in the Introduction, I am the president of my local investment association. We meet twice monthly and keep things as informal as possible. For example, at the beginning of every meeting we have a deal session where investors can come to talk about and exchange deals. Investors can come just for the deal session or choose to stay for the entire meeting. We are also planning to do monthly property tours. This not only is an opportunity for the property owner to make a deal but it acts as a teaching tool as well. Even seasoned investors can learn something new by touring properties in markets that are unfamiliar to them.

Networking is the power of many—many focuses, many ideas, many motivations. It goes in conjunction with an investor's education. While investors can learn a great deal from books, seminars, and training courses, it is through networking, through doing, where investors learn how to apply what they were taught in a seminar. Often when you read something, you can't get clarity about the subject without networking. You can't validate what you have read.

Find avenues to learn and network. Find opportunities to volunteer for tasks. I want to be the resource for all the things my investors want or need. I can find them tenants, or do open houses. Volunteering is a free education. All it takes is some of your time, yet you get to hang around and learn from someone else.

Ask people in what markets they would like to buy, and then go out and find properties. If you do the legwork, they will reciprocate by letting you watch them go through the process and learn from their experience. Help more people get what they want and you will always get what you want. You will build rapport, repeat business, and opportunities.

As I mentioned earlier, networking can also help you build your team. Having the right people in the right positions is essential to achieving your goals. The likelihood of meeting the appropriate person for the position you need to fill, whether it's a bookkeeper or real estate agent, will increase through networking.

Building Your Team

Just like many investors, when I first got into real estate investing, I tried to do everything myself. Doing everything yourself means you don't have to spend the money to hire someone else, right? It's better for your bottom line. Well, not necessarily when you consider what your time is worth.

For example, if I need my lawn mowed, I can certainly go out and cut the grass myself. I have the equipment and I would save myself the cost of hiring the task out, but is it really worth my time? Is the ten dollars I would save by not hiring the kid down the street, who would probably cut the grass more quickly than I could, really worth an hour or so of my time? Definitely not. I might be out ten bucks, but my grass would be cut and I would have been able to use that hour doing something only I am able to do.

It's important to differentiate between whether a specific task needs to be done by you or if someone else can do it. Many investors who are just starting out feel that their time is worth everything, so they have to do everything themselves, but I say that's bull. Don't be afraid to delegate. Unless you are doing something because you enjoy it or you are doing it to relax, you don't need to be the one to do it.

Having the right people in the right positions is essential to success and achieving goals. By delegating whatever you can, you will free up your time to focus on the things only you can do. If a task is not important for you to do, then it's important for you to not do it. There will always be someone else who can do it. When you hire the right people, the task is not only done correctly, it will often be done better than you could have done it. You might think not hiring that plumber or electrician and doing the work yourself is a huge cost savings until something goes wrong and you have to hire a professional anyway.

When it comes to hiring the right people for the right positions, my advice is to trust your instincts. Human beings are natural doers. We like to do things. We want to help. We want to support everybody. We want to be of assistance, but sometimes trying to do everything hinders creativity. It's important to figure out what tasks only you can do and what needs to get done first.

In the Marine Corp, our first priority was troop welfare. Second to that is mission accomplishment. In other words, it is more important to take care of our people first then accomplish the mission. You can't accomplish the mission if you don't have the right manpower. If your support network—your staff, clients, or family—is not taken care of, they won't be able to help you reach your goals.

A common mentality is to just go for it and worry about the consequences later. Often people will simply fall back and retreat whenever they can't accomplish the mission or goal, instead of focusing on building their team first. You don't need a lot of people in your team, just the right people.

In the Marine Corp, our battalions are small. You can't be swift, silently, and deadly with a large troop base, and often it doesn't take a ton of people to accomplish a mission. It just takes proper delegation and focusing on the right person for the task. Think of it like quality over quantity.

So, how do you find the right person for a position or task? Well, you really have to be good at reading personalities. Certain personalities are good fits for some roles and poor fits for others. It is only through being able to read personalities that you can tell if a candidate is a good fit or not. For example, an analytical role needs to be filled by analytically-minded person, someone who is by-the-book, so to speak.

There are four basic personality types, known as DISC for short:

D = Dominant – an active type, someone with this personality is task-oriented. They can often be rigid but gets things done in a hurry.

I = Influential – an active type, someone with this personality is people-oriented. They would be a good fit for a sales position. While they aren't usually leadership material, they aren't bottom of the pack either.

S = Steady – a passive type, someone with this personality is people-oriented. They are supporters and caretakers, and are often nurturing.

C = Conscientious – a passive type, someone with this personality is task-oriented. They would be a good fit for an accounting position.

Not everyone fits squarely into one of these four types. Often combinations of personalities can be ideal for specific positions. For example, true perfection in sales would be someone who is a combination of I and D personality types. For growth positions such as budgeting and finance, you want to look for someone better than you. Administrators should be good supporters and good listeners. For the ideal project manager, you would want someone who is rigid and focused on their trade. Definitely look for someone who has experience in your market.

For marketing positions, you need someone who is fun, but also focused on growth. They should be a people-person and love to win challenges. When it comes to personal assistants, you really want someone who will be harder on you than you are on yourself. They need a drill instructor mentality, have a logistical mind and exceptional organizational skills.

Overall, you really need to have people who challenge you on your team. If they aren't challenging you, they aren't going to help you achieve your goals. A good piece of advice is to be quick to fire, slow to hire. You can't go down the path of imperfection for long before it becomes bad for business.

Making sure your subordinates are managing their teams and that it goes down the tree.

If it's not important to say, it's important not to say it. There is a time to listen to what you want more than what I want. Same thing in habits and doing.

MOE MATTHEWS BIO:

MY NAME is Moe Mathews. I am primarily a Single Family, Affordable Housing Investor, developer of Assisted Living Homes Owner of a 501 C3 called Veterans Path Up Richmond Virginia Inc based out of the Hanover, VA area. I am looking to connect with Deals and Deal Makers in all areas I do business in as a HomeVestors®, We Buy Ugly Houses® Franchise in Richmond VA, Chattanooga, TN and Jackson MS. Make sure to Friend me on social media, and Like my Connected Investors profile. You can reach me at 804-295-0000 or by visiting http://www.moemathews.com.

Here is my Background:

Moe was raised in the West End of Richmond and graduated from Douglas Freeman High School, and then he joined the United States Marine Corps.

Moe quickly became a highly decorated war veteran and in 1999, as a Staff Sergeant he was selected at the age of 29, as the youngest Warrant Officer in the entire Marine Corps.

Moe received his education from University of Maryland while on active duty in Okinawa, Japan with his family. After serving 13 honorable years in the Marine Corps Moe started a successful and thriving marketing and advertising company called bMessages, Inc.

Moe is currently Co-Owner / Manager of Fresh Start Property Solutions LLC, Affordable Housing Partners LLC & ReFresh Investments LLC which are HomeVestors® Franchises (We Buy The Good, The Bad, The Ugly Houses®), Fresh Start Group LLC, Fresh Start Renovations, LLC, Fresh Start Realty LLC, and co-owner of Fresh Start Team that is Brokered by eXp Realty LLC.

Moe is married to Cathy who is also an Associate Broker and team manager the Fresh Start Team that is Brokered by eXp Realty which is the fastest growing, agent owned Real Estate Brokerage in the world today. They have two children, both graduates of Virginia Commonwealth University.

As a Realtor and Investor for many years Moe enjoys working with Buyers, Seller and Investors who are mostly referrals from happy clients.

To gain access to my Wholesaling Live Course, Learn how to turn Change into Serious Cash and gain access to our tips videos and training content for all things Real Estate visit my site and join our members area at http://www.moemathews.com or http://www.freshstartinvestors.com